CHANGING OF THE GUARD
THE RISING OF GENERATION

Xtreme

Rev. Carl Wesley Anderson, Jr., M.Div.

www.borntoblaze.com email: info@borntoblaze.com

"...the glory of the LORD will rise
upon you. And nations will come to your light, and kings
to the brightness of your rising." Isaiah 60:2b-3

Lord, we stand here as a desperate people, hungry
for the things of you.

Come quiet the storms that rage all around us so
that we hear the passion that beats through your
heart.

Spirit, put healing in our hands, put life in our
words, and drive a passion for the lost deep in the
hearts of your people.

Inhabit the praises of us, your children,
and Father, send us out with a reckless passion.
Deliver us from evil, and set a standard of unity
to break down walls and to heal your people.
Unity is the cry of your church, Lord. Reconcile the
children to the fathers, and with forgiveness and
mercy, rush through the hearts of our land.

We cry out our deep need for you, Jesus. Oh God,
come in power and bring glory to your name..[1]

—*A spontaneous prayer from a young woman for our
Generation during the live worship event,
"The Road to One Day", 2000.*

Changing of the Guard: the Rising of Generation Xtreme
Copyright © 2005 by Carl Wesley Anderson, Jr.
Original Draft completed December 24, 1995.

For additional copies, please visit www.borntoblaze.com

Born to Blaze Ministries Mission Statement: *"An International Outreach to Call People to Repentance and Inspire Believers to Passionate Discipleship."*

Unless otherwise indicated, Scripture taken from the NEW AMERICAN STANDARD BIBLE, copyright 1960, 1962, 1963, 1968, 1971, 1972, 1973, 1975, 1977, by the Lockman Foundation. Used by permission.

Edited by Karin Miller. Cover design by Suzann Beck, BeckHaus Design, Inc.

To obtain permission, please write to: Born to Blaze Ministries, P.O. Box 46105, Plymouth, Minnesota, 55446, U.S.A.

Printed in the United States of America by Bethany Press International.
ISBN: 0-9762910-0-2

Dedication & Thank You

A special "thank you" to my tireless editor, Karen Miller, (*who caused me to re-think and re-work nearly every page from 1995 in this book!*), Suzann Beck for her awesome cover design, and Dr. Lance Wonders for his thought-provoking Preface.

To my natural and spiritual parents and relationships, the mentors who sacrificially took the time to help me carve out and discover my path to life in Jesus Christ. I honor you.

To my flawless wife Sarah Elizabeth, the wife of my youth, without whom I would be a wreck. You are my sweet.
I thank you for your continuous support and encouragement.

And to my two sons, Ethan Whitefield and Gideon Wesley; the true next generation I am responsible for helping raise up. I pour out my life for you. May you run faster and run farther than your daddy ever did.

"Each age, it is found, must write its own books;
or rather, each generation for the next succeeding.
The books of an older period will not fit this."[2]

CONTENTS

Contents

PREFACE TO
CHANGING OF THE GUARD

Carl Anderson is right – Generation X is indeed a generation of great destiny!

As Carl transposes the "X" of this title from the English "X" – a supposed "unknown quantity" – into the Greek "X" – the letter "Chi" which functions like a "ch" in English and is the first letter in "Christos" or "Christ" – he claims a special relationship between this generation and its returning Lord.

Interestingly, the Two Witnesses of Revelations 11, who prepare the way for the Lord's return in the last days, are modeled after Moses and Elijah – two figures who are prominently featured in this book as biblical examples of mentors. Moses and Elijah were mentors of Joshua and Elisha respectively, who went beyond them by God's grace and brought their ministries to completion. If Carl is correct in his metaphors, then it becomes *good news* that if and when the "old guard" Moseses and Elijahs finish up their work by passing the baton to a whole "new guard" of Joshuas and Elishas, they will be endued by God with a "double-portion" of His Spirit.

Nevertheless, as Carl points out, this "generation of destiny" has drawn the Enemy's attacks. First, there has been the attempt to destroy it physically before it is even born via abortion; secondly, there has been an attempt to rob it socially of its necessary nurture from "fathers" and "mothers;" and thirdly, there has been an attempt to twist it philosophically by muddying its backdrop of faith via secularism, relativism, pluralism, and post-modernism. Thus, even if this generation is born physically, it will be incredibly difficult for it to be "reborn" and "grow up" spiritually and intellectually to have any measure of practical influence in a world that "remembers not Joseph" – nor Moses, Elijah, nor even Jesus Christ Himself.

The Lord seems to have chosen to pour out the same pre-planned measure of His Spirit upon this generation; however, with fewer "vessels" or "instruments" to do His work, He then pours that much *more* of His Spirit into the life of each one who is willing to be used! Thus, instead of dispensing billions of warriors with a little bit of His Spirit, He fills hundreds of thousands (even millions?) worldwide with a *great deal* of His Spirit who will be *more* intense, *more* committed, and *more* radical than the average Christian in the average generation has ever been before!

Even with this book's strong focus on the Joshua generation, thankfully, Carl also foresees a place for the Moseses (like yours truly) of the "old guard" who have a "different spirit" in them (a Joshua/Caleb spirit, yet aged as the Moses generation) and can be useful partners in this last-days (or at least next-to-last days) work. Hopefully, we can cover our more youthful partners while they are more often on the frontlines and taking the greater risks.

Carl also emphasizes the importance of "intimacy" with God, who is experienced as a true Father, but also as one with "motherly" compassion. In an era of distant and sometimes self-absorbed, workaholic, or performance-oriented fathers and mothers, the Lord Himself – along with His Church, our "mother" through the Spirit – must fill a lot of holes in our souls.

Mentors are a significant means for this to happen, although sometimes God alone is fully able to make up the difference of what has been lost.

Behind the scenes, Carl seeks to fully live out the challenge he brings to you in these pages. He is a "prophet" of sorts – moreso in the "exhorter" and "encourager" modes than in the "reading of hearts" or "prediction of the future" modes, though the Lord occasionally uses him in the latter modes as well. He is a student of history – *salvation history* – not simply to collect more facts, but in order to quicken and inform his own faith, since the God who did mighty wonders in the past is the same God today!

Carl's style is passionate, anecdotal, and eclectic – but there is rhythm, rhyme, and reason in what he gives us here as well. This is a "living" essay, rather than a dead and dissected theological treatise, yet there is good theology in here as well! Even "old" theologians like myself can find fresh bread in many of these insights!

May the Lord truly use this book as a manual of inspiration to Gen-X'ers of *whatever* age, to stand together and finish the task of restoration, harvest, and daily laying down our lives in obedient witness until He comes again. Whether or not it ever becomes a best-seller is in the Lord's hands, but may it fall into the hands and hearts of the *right* fellow-soldiers who can understand, appreciate, and put into practice the vision that our brother describes.

To God alone be the glory, both now and until the King and the Kingdom come in full measure, and may we be found faithful until that proper time. Amen and Amen.

Dr. Lance Wonders
October 30, 2004

THESE TIMES DEMAND
A SPECIAL RESPONSE

"Then Caleb quieted the people before Moses,
and said, 'We should by all means go up
and take possession of it,
for we shall surely overcome it.'"

— *Numbers 13:30*

THESE TIMES DEMAND A RESPONSE

This book is unique. Apart from the following introductory remarks (and a thorough re-write after a recent editing) it was composed almost entirely in an intense five-day period toward the end of 1995, as a prophetic *voice* from the Lord, a call to ignite spiritual passion and cast vision for a whole generation that the world and the church has written off.

What has followed these past nine or ten years has been *the echo*. It has been an echo of confirmation both in the secular world as well as the realm of the Church, and the time is now for this book to enter widespread distribution. In other words, this book is rare in that it was written and finished some years before many other voices and ministries were raised up in the heartbeat of God to begin to impact the young generation. And this introduction will document some of the 'echo's' that have resounded over the past nine or ten years in confirmation of the 'voice' of this work.

What you are about to read in the chapters ahead is a combination of prophetic seeds that I had received from the Lord during the years 1990-1995, while I was a young spiritual cadet and apprentice in my early twenties. During that time I was mentored by a special group of spiritual fathers, mothers, uncles, & aunts and ministered evangelistically throughout America, Europe, and Asia. Back then, I felt this vision was going to be significant within a few years, perhaps the late 1990's or early 2000's. So I finished the book in December 1995, put it away, dug in my trenches, and waited. Soon it would be time for the Changing of the Guard.

What was I waiting for? I needed confirmation from other leaders around the world that "my generation" was indeed to be special for the end times before I could cast broader vision. Would other leaders, young and old, see what I was seeing? The older generation is passing away; the anointing to go further is upon the youth of my generation. The Guard has changed. Moses is dead, and Joshua is alive. The baton has passed from the old to the new. This book is also unique in that it is written from an X'er to X'ers and mentors, from an X'er's prophetic perspective.

Why is this book important? A recent study, conducted in 2002 by Research International, a market research bureau, polled diverse Generation X'ers working for a variety of companies in

IT IS IMPERATIVE FOR MEMBERS OF OUR GENERATION TO KNOW THE BIGGER PICTURE

the marketplace and stumbled upon an amazing truth. They realized that to keep an X'er on board, you must share with them that they are part of a larger whole. They must know how they connect to the broad vision of what they are doing, rather than keeping them stifled in one particular skill. It is imperative for members of our generation to know the bigger picture; therefore, a pioneer is needed to cast the vision so we each know how our little piece fits into the greater whole. Nine years ago I was such a pioneer, and the time has come for this book to join other such pioneers in describing the big picture of God's last days purpose for Generation X.

In his book, Inspire the Fire, Ron Luce, a modern day Moses to this Joshua generation, shares, "The excitement of the world won't make the young generation zealous for the Lord. The only things that will maintain genuine spiritual fervor are purpose, commitment and a sense of belonging to something greater than anything this world offers."[3]It is with this in mind that the following book was written. It is meant to be a spark in your spiritual fireplace, a fuel added to your smoldering embers to ignite a larger flame of passion and purpose for our generation.

WHO IS GENERATION X?

Let's define our terminology. "Our generation" - what is that? I was born in 1970, just three years before the Supreme Court of the United States legalized abortion. My parents were both born in the 1930's and grew up in a generation that has been termed the G.I. generation. The Great Depression and WWII shaped them. Next came the so-called Baby Boomers, those born in about 1940-60. The Vietnam War and the Watergate scandal shaped them. Then we come to what has been termed, "Generation X." Many statistical references set the years of birth at about 1962-82.

Let me diverge from normal worldly thinking for the vision of this book. In God's terms, a "generation" lasts for forty years. The generation of people which abandoned God in the wilderness and were left to die there lasted forty years. Only after forty years were complete was the new generation allowed to rise up and take the land. The number forty itself is significant throughout the scriptures. For example, Moses spent forty days on the mountain, receiving the law of God, and Jesus spent forty days fasting in the wilderness, completing a significant testing period and then entering into the fullness of the Spirit. Both of these periods of forty were symbolic of a complete period of time. The actual Hebrew word for, "generation" means, "a revolution of times."

So for our purposes in this book, we are going to define "Generation X" as anyone born in the approximate years 1960-2000; that's forty years of babies and a whole lot of people!

There are other terms being given to those born more recently, such as, "Bridgers" and "Millenials," but I feel that God's purpose is to put an anointing on a massive number of young people, encompassing even some being born at this time.

So when you read the term Generation X in the following pages, be thinking in God's terms of a forty year period and not in terms of a twenty year period. Interestingly, you can ask anyone in their 30's, 20's, or teens today where they were when they heard about the Columbine shootings or 9/11 and they can tell you. The previous generations had the assassination of Kennedy or the Atomic Bomb on Hiroshima as moments of personal impact.[4]

We will be using various terms in this book to define the same generation, Generation X, we are currently addressing. One of these terms is, "Joshua Generation." It may benefit the reader to take a few minutes and read over some passages of scripture

JOSHUA ROSE UP AND LED OTHER YOUNG WARRIORS TO POSSESS THE LAND THAT GOD HAD PROMISED IN THE PREVIOUS GENERATION

which point to the relationship, calling, and equipping of Joshua through the ministry of Moses which are found in Exodus and Deuteronomy. The reason we use the term "Joshua Generation," is that Joshua, a leader of strength and training under Moses, rose up and led other young warriors to possess the land that God had promised in the previous generation. Some of these passages include Exodus 24:13-18, 33:7-11, and Deuteronomy 31:7-29.

We will also be using the terms, "Generation Yes," "Generation Extreme," "Generation Miraculous," "Generation For Jesus," and, "Generation Destruction." All of these terms fit the same period of time of which even the author himself and his children were born into: about 1962 to 2002, give or take a couple of years. The, "Joshua Generation" and Generation X are synonymous with all these terms in this book.

To sum up, this book is targeted to two main groups of warriors....first to those under forty years of age, born between 1960-2000 or so, the "Joshua's," and to those born before about 1960, the "Moses'." For the "Joshua Generation," you will be challenged and filled with inspirational vision to carry you forward in your growth in God. For the "Moses Generation," you will gain valuable insight into the youth of our culture, and fresh understanding of "what makes us tick." What is the vision of God for us in this hour? How does our culture relate to each other and especially to you? How can you relate and pass on the wisdom you have gained and be heard and understood by us? These and many other themes will be discussed in the following pages.

It is to many of the youth (all those aged about 40 years old and younger), that God is granting unique authority in this hour. He is granting it to those who would choose to respond when their name is called from among the ranks to serve Him and walk in Gospel Power. In one sense, to any of any age who would choose to swim against the stream of tradition and seek Him for fresh direction; to any of any age who would respond to a call to advance the Kingdom in a path that's never been tread before. This includes both generations, Moses and Joshua.

Once again, this introduction is meant to spur you on to see how the original revelation given to the author in the early 1990's is a voice which has been echoed sufficiently to be released with urgency for the current decade or two ahead. This brings us to the first in a series of "echo-type" confirmations about the timing of this book and the call to our generation to arise and do great exploits in the name of Christ.

The following are some prophetic 'echo's' to the original 'voice' of this publication. They include a couple of book references which the author has included in the appendix under 'Ministry Resources' as well as a number of testimonies and emails.

"CONFIRMATIONS"

In this introduction, I will quote a variety of sources which con-firm the themes composed back in 1994-1995. Space will not permit a complete compilation, but know that there are hundreds of leaders and ministries who have hearts and callings to also come alongside the radical uprising of our generation. I will assemble them in chronological order.

Even earlier in the decade of the 1990's, God was speaking. In a vision from John Yemma, Generation X leader from the Vineyard Movement, dated July 18, 1991, he shares,

"The Lord is telling me He is going to reform youth ministry as we know it...he is going to place the anointing for youth min-istry in the hands of the youth themselves. They will do the ministry of Jesus. The Lord will do miracles through the youth, they will disciple those friends who come to Jesus and great waves of anointing will flow from them. No worldliness will be found in them; they will walk holy and pure with their God. Some will be persecuted...for their radical stand for Jesus. 'Follow Me,' says the Lord, 'Follow Me as I gather millions of young people to love me only and serve their God.' Sons will be brought back to fathers and fathers to sons, and the same shall be for daughters. This generation shall not only raise the spiritually dead but shall also see the physical resurrection power of God."[5]

Back in 1996, Rick Joyner had a remarkable vision. He writes, "I saw multitudes of young people, black and white together, marching and demonstrating. They all carried banners but there was nothing written on them. I then heard a voice from heaven saying, 'Who will give them their cause?' I saw a long line of men

THE YOUTH ARE GOING TO BE MOBILIZED AGAIN, AND THEY ARE WAITING FOR A CAUSE

and women waiting to speak to the crowd. They represented many different causes, but to my shock most of them were Nazis. I then felt a gripping urgency to speak to this great crowd before they did." He explained the application, "The youth are going to be mobilized again, and they are waiting for a cause. They will respond to radical Christianity, but they will be repulsed by watered-down versions. If the church does not fill the void in youth that demands a cause, they will turn to a power that will mobilize them for the most sinister reasons."[6]

In 1998 another prophetic word burst forth on the email lists from Irene Mederos. "There is a new generation that is catching on to this fresh flame; a new breed of God's chosen to do mighty exploits in His name. It's not only a sound of music but also a cry of the Spirit in the wilderness preparing the way of the Lord for end-time harvest. It is the cry of the Spirit in the spirit of Elisha, picking up Elijah's mantle with a double portion anointing. This new generation is a prophetic bunch of revolutionaries that are dissatisfied and tired of the same 'ol, same 'ol. They are warriors, defiant against Satan. One by one, they are catching the vision, writing it down, and running with it and nothing will be able to stop them because God's power, anointing, and authority is on them."[7]

Even in the realm of the natural, this great plan of God to put a special purpose on an entire generation is being confirmed. The shaking that is happening is effecting both natural and spiritual realms. In August of 1998 there was a special gathering of young Gen. X leaders in their twenties, many of whom were not Christians. Duke University brought together fifty of the brightest minds of the next generation of leaders together. They formed a document labeled, "The Content of Our Character: Voices of Generation X." In it, they wrote, "We gathered to share ideals with one another and begin to construct our vision for this American generation. We strive to honor the enlightened values that forged this country, and we further propose new ideals that echo what Vaclav Havel describes as our 'higher responsibility.'"[8]

This great shift in the Spirit realm is affecting even the political and natural realms for our generation! If the world system itself can jump on the band wagon and begin to recognize the tremendous need in this hour for a 'higher responsibility,' then so can we, the Church.

One of the greatest pointers in our time of this great uprising of passion and purpose is the music that God is bringing to change praise and worship forever. Again, space would not permit listing the many passionate worship leaders and song writers God has raised up in the past ten years, and the many number that will be raised up in the years to come. Louie Giglio of Atlanta, Georgia has been a key leader organizing a vision of passionate worship and worship leaders to our generation. Birthed in 1995, the vision has seen the organization of huge gatherings of young people called "Passion." These gatherings continue to grow every year. In a recent journal entry from his website, he poetically writes,

"While we yet have time, we must ask God to riddle our pride.
 While we still can, we must consider the cost.
 While day lingers, we must work as if night is coming.
 While the world sleeps, we must heighten our senses.
 While most waste away, we must renew within.
 While earth settles down, we must continually look up.
 While many fear death, we must embrace life.
 While others play it safe, we must risk it all."[9]

"Sometime in the first half of 1999, something snapped," writes Dr. Michael Brown in his preface to Revolution! A Call to Holy War. "Perhaps it was the Columbine killings; perhaps it was the accumulated frustration mounting from years of political corruption and moral decline in America; perhaps it was the realization that the American Church had gone as far as it could with its present mind-set and methods. Whatever the exact factors were, I am sure of this: Believers across the land began to say, "Enough is enough. We need a revolution!"[10] The Brownsville School of Revival, alongside another training center where Dr. Brown teaches, has trained thousands for radical faith in the past few years. His book is a marvelous compilation of themes around the holy revolution that is sweeping our nation; it is a must read.

In the last chapter of this book, under the heading, "Passing the Baton," I prophetically talk about the death of certain individuals who will birth this new thing, kind of like the idea that it was only after Moses died, representing the last of the previous generation, that Joshua arose to take the land. The death of the old is the birth of the new.

In an email dated August 8, 1999, entitled, "The Torch Has Passed," David Works gives a synopsis of the funeral of young Rachel Scott. She became a martyr and hero to our generation when she faced a gunman in her school and died for her faith. At her funeral, Pastor Bruce Porter asked the young people present how many would pick up the torch that Rachel carried. The response was incredible. "Hundreds rose up and said, "Yes!" Kent Henry led worship; then powerful testimonies were given by Ron Luce, Bob Weiner, Josh Weidman, and Melody Green. Cindy Jacobs also shared that she sensed prophetically that the way to avenge the blood of the martyrs is to bring in as many new souls as possible into the Kingdom. Her sense was that there is a special place in this revival for young girls and that it will be marked by the sign of raising people from the dead."[11]

In a unique email message entitled "Generation Yes," Bobby Conner prophetically shares how the death of young martyr Cassie Bernall, who on the morning of April 20, 1999 was gunned down in the Columbine shooting, is a sign that God is raising a whole generation like her, who say "Yes" to Jesus no matter what the cost. A year earlier sixteen year-old Cassie wrote, "I will die for my God. I will die for my faith. It's the least I can do for Christ dying for me." Conner writes, "The end-times generation will live life passionately with an all-or-nothing attitude. They will give the yes of someone who truly believes they have found something worth living for. They will say yes to God with a zeal that amazes older believers and overcomes the world. God is releasing upon this upcoming generation a passion for the presence of the Lord. It is this passion that will allow them to be filled with such a resolve."[12] In 1994, God also gave me personal confirmation of this word. I will share it with you in the first section of this book under the heading: "Generation X…Generation Yes."

A GENERATION BEING BORN

Returning for a moment to Bobby Conner, in another email message printed in 1999, he shares, "There is coming a world-wide youth revival, the Spirit of God will release such 'passion' for the presence of the Lord. This coming awakening will sweep across the earth, like a wild fire, nothing will be able to stop, nor stand in the way. These youth will begin to come together in the year 2000, and by the year 2002 they will be on the move. Their message will be the words of Micah 3:8 'But as for

BUT AS FOR ME, I AM FILLED WITH POWER, WITH THE SPIRIT OF THE LORD

me, I am filled with power, with the Spirit of the Lord, and with justice and might, to declare to Jacob his transgression, and to Israel his sin.'" (NIV)[13]

In another email message from 1999, Catherine Brown from Scotland saw a similar picture. "I saw a vision of the earth split-ting wide open and one by one, young men and women were attempting to come forth from creation. As I looked more close-ly, I saw that there was a covering over the place where the young people were trying to come out of. It had the appearance of an amniotic sac and the young people were struggling to push their way out. I immediately was impressed by the Spirit that this was a birthing process and that it was a difficult birth. I heard the Spirit say, 'Push, Church, Push.' Simultaneously with this vision, I saw a vision of the Lord, and from the center of His being, many young people were running out from Him. From the womb of the dawn the warriors came forth."[14]

Around this same period of time, Randy Clarke's ministry spread and caused dozens of ministries to sprout up with a focus on releasing the younger generation in the power of the Spirit. Among them was Global X-Stream with vision to impart and train the youth in the anointing of the Spirit.

In November of 1999 a group of apostolic and prophetic elders under the leadership of C. Peter Wagner, met in Colorado Springs. One of the reports that was given is as follows: "A great youth revival is coming to America. Schools will be shaken for the glory of God. Many young people will be drawn into the church as they were during the Jesus movement. God warned us that we must be ready to receive them or we might miss this move of God."[15]

Also in late 1999, God put a spirit of passion into Pastor Che Ahn, Lou Engle, and a group of other key leaders from around the country to launch a cooperative effort to fill the Capitol Mall with 1,000,000 youth in Washington D.C. This event was appropriately named, "The Call DC." Hundreds of thousands of youth responded when the event was organized in 2000, and this was followed later that year by a forty day fast in which thousands of youth participated in. A true awakening had begun. Similar gatherings took place in the last few years in New York, Texas, California, and other states. Since then streams of leaders have begun assembling together. One example is Mike Bickle from International House of Prayer (IHOP) in Kansas City, linking together with Che Ahn and Lou Engle for synergy to ignite Generation X through special annual conferences like "One Thing" and "The Call."

YOUR OLD MEN WILL SEE VISIONS,
YOUR YOUNG MEN WILL DREAM DREAMS

Bob Jones and Keith Davis, in their newsletter entitled, "Shepherd's Rod 2001," begin by quoting Psalm 4 and sharing, "There will be a measurable increase in the anointing falling upon young people. Bob was awakened at 4:00 a.m. and informed by a vision from the Holy Spirit that Psalm 4 specifically applied to the youth. In the vision, he saw large gatherings of young people whose character and nature was being forged and molded into the very image of Christ, thus imparting His divine nature qualifying them to carry the powerful anointing promised in the days ahead."[16]

You see, the old men dream dreams of what has been already; they ponder the glory years of the campaigns already fought and the bat-

THERE WILL BE A MEASURABLE INCREASE IN THE ANOINTING FALLING UPON YOUNG PEOPLE

tles already won. The "young men" (and, of course, "young women") see visions - visions of what is yet possible for their own generation if they put their hand to the plow and never look back.

Finally, in the long list of potential email confirmations from hundreds of various entries, are three that are strong confirmations of the title and message of this book. First, evangelist Todd Bentley, an X'er himself in his twenties, wrote a fascinating message entitled, "Generation Miraculous." He contends, "I believe that Generation X is a parallel to Joshua and Caleb who tasted of the fruit of the vine and were no longer satisfied with unbelief but wanted the full destiny of God. It was in this move of the river that many X'ers were greatly impacted and saved. There have been a few of this generation to really abandon themselves to God and be a voice of revival; for whatever reason we only have the first-fruits. I was praying into the destiny of this generation and God said their purpose is the gospel with power miraculous. We will cross the Jordan, stir the church out of unbelief and make them hungry for what we tasted; God will release new preaching anointing and music with new songs being birthed out of heavenly experiences. We are crossing the Jordan into a new day."[17]

CHANGING OF THE GUARD

The two final prophetic words directly confirm the title of this book, Changing of the Guard, which was named in 1995. They are two 'echo-type' confirmations of the voice of destiny in the following chapters. First, from Dave Bodine in May of 2000. "Yesterday I heard the Holy Spirit say, "divine realignment" and "changing of the guards." This is going to bring much change. Divine order will come forth…a holy fear will come once again upon the church of Jesus Christ."[18]

The second one comes from the fateful morning of September 11, 2001, when terrorism would forever shake the country of America. Phil Buekler, himself a Moses-style mentor to Generation X, was in an early morning prayer meeting at his church, and heard these words from the Spirit, "This is the changing of the guard. I am transforming the leadership in this country from the wicked to the righteous." Phil understood the application of this to include the political and social realms as well as the spiritual at the time, but the word the Lord gave him is also a powerful confirmation of the title and message of this book. It is now high time for the change. The old must move over, and make room for the new. The Guard is changing.

It is time for us as the next generation to arise and go forth, for the Lord our God is with us. Moses is dead. "Now arise, and cross this Jordan." The key is, we must start now. Martin Luther's godly mentor, Spalatin, once counseled Luther on the importance of immediacy in making decisions and acting firmly upon them. He remarked to Luther, "Don't put off 'till tomorrow! By delay Hannibal lost Rome. By delay Esau forfeited his birthright. Christ said, 'Ye shall seek me, and ye shall not find.' Thus scripture, experience, and all creation testify that the gifts of God must be taken on the wing."[19]

Here's a summary of the key issues I feel God is wanting to bring to the forefront in this book. There are three main sections. The first contains the issues of who we are as a generation. It is visionary in aspect. I examine themes of: the attack of Satan upon previous generations which were unique in God's timetable, and his attack on this current generation through abortion, secularism, and the fatherless aspect of our generation. I look at the characteristics of our generation and how we respond to life. I quote various statistics from publications which give data necessary to understanding our generation, and also share some stories from church history of young people who lived in parallel worlds of darkness like ours but decided to cast off the works of darkness and embrace the armor of light. I use inspiring historical examples of others God has used significantly. What Satan and man have planned for evil God will turn around for good. Our greatest weaknesses as a generation are also our greatest strengths.

The second section is geared toward Gen. Xer's and also helpful to any of the "Moses Generation" who want to know who we are in light of our identity as being in The Father, and that, by the Spirit, the church herself is positioned by God to be our "mother". Too many in our generation have lacked the fullness of a father and mother figure, and the two chapters in this section shed light on our unique place as sons and daughters of the Almighty. I share various truths and weave them together from both scriptural and personal examples.

The third section is more practical, with the theme of living a radical lifestyle for Jesus in spite of the culture around us. The themes of character, apprenticeship and mentoring, responding to the call and going into ministry on any level are included. This section will also be helpful to those who are Moseses as it gives scriptural and historical examples of proper mentoring and apprenticing and what works and doesn't work in affecting our generation for the gospel. Mentoring is fast becoming a buzz word for our time.

I close the book with a challenge and then add some helpful resources in the appendixes. My aim is to introduce a number of themes and weave them together into this great vision of following Christ in a radical way in our generation, and how we are connected in the plan of God to usher in the very end of days. The other authors listed at the back have fuller resources available which teach and describe the themes covered more fully.

A Torch is Being Passed To Light the Dark Places

As a final confirmation to the themes of this book, I will share a few quotes. Arnold Dallimore once wrote a special two-volume set on the life and times of evangelist George Whitefield. I write more about him in the fourth chapter of this book, as he was perhaps the best known household name of his own generation. He started preaching at age twenty-one, and blazed a trail of field preaching that hundreds followed in the next generation. Now long dead, his life and testimony continue. As you read this quote, please note that it applies to young men and young women alike and be stirred. Dallimore writes,

"Yea, this book is written in the desire—perhaps in a measure of inner certainty—that we shall see the great Head of the Church once more bring into being His special instruments of revival, that He will again raise up unto Himself certain young men and women whom He may use in this glorious employment. And what manner of men will they be? Those mighty in the majesty and holiness of God, and their minds and hearts aglow with the great truths of the doctrines of grace. They will be those who have learned what it is to die to self, to human aims and personal ambitions; those who are willing to be 'fools for Christ's sake,' who will bear reproach and falsehood, who will labor and suffer, and whose supreme desire will be, not to gain earth's accolades, but to win the Master's approbation when they appear before His awesome judgment seat. They will be those who will preach with broken hearts and tear-filled eyes, and upon whose ministries God will grant an extraordinary effusion of the Holy Spirit, and who will witness 'signs and wonders following' in the transformation of multitudes of human lives."[20]

Wow! <u>The times in which we live demand a special response.</u> The stakes are higher now; it is a life and death proposal for some. Who will take up the torch that is now passed to our generation? Who will stand in this wicked and perverse world, a world grown dark through dead formalistic religion and secular humanism, where anyone who rises above the status quo will be considered foolish and narrow-minded? <u>Will you seek to exercise a fuller confidence in God's word and His power than the previous generations?</u> "Christians," said Luther, "must have the vision which enables them to disregard the terrible spectacle and outward appearance, the devil and the guns of the whole world, and to see Him who sits on high and says: 'I am the One who spoke to you.'"[21a]

The Psalmist wrote, *"Walk about Zion, and go around her; count her towers; consider her ramparts; go through her palaces; that you may tell it to the next generation." Psalm 48:12-13.* I have been on a short walk around her towers, and what I have seen I will tell you now. It is only a portion of the bigger whole of what God is saying to His Church in these last days. Yet it is an important tower to enter and explore. Let each chapter be another level of this tower of the Lord's fortress of Zion, for you are the next generation and if you don't conquer the promised land as the Joshua and Caleb Generation, we'll have to wait another forty years of wandering in this wilderness.

In closing of these introductory remarks, in November of 2003 I found myself ministering to a group in Chichester, England; a city where a radical 24-7 prayer and outreach movement began in 1999 by visionary leader Pete Grieg and a group of Gen. Xer's, one of whom I met. A book recently published entitled, Red Moon Rising (listed in my Appendix as a must-read) describes the whole movement in awesome narrative detail. Currently, there are places with 24 hour-a-day, 7 day-a-week prayer in over 50 nations! Early one morning, inspired by the Spirit, Pete sat down during a prayer slot and penned the poetic piece, *"The Vision."* In a portion of it he writes,

> "Don't you hear them coming? Herald the weirdos!
> Summon the losers and the freaks.
> Here come the frightened and forgotten with fire in their
> eyes.
> They walk tall and trees applaud, skyscrapers bow, moun-
> tains are dwarfed by these
> children of another dimension.
> Their prayers summon the hounds of heaven & invoke the
> ancient dream of Eden.
> And this vision will be. It will come to pass; it will come
> easily; it will come soon." [21b]

So the echo of revelatory confirmation to the changing of the guard is spreading throughout the earth. As you read the following pages, consider,

Who among you, young and old, will be a flaming torch, with fire in your eyes, to dispel the darkness? Will you?...

–*Reverend Carl Wesley Anderson, Jr., October 25, 2004,*
Soli Deo Gloria.

X MARKS THE SPOT

"Once to every man and nation,
Comes the moment to decide
In the strife of truth with falsehood,
For the good or evil side."

— *James Russell*

CHAPTER ONE

GENERATION DESTRUCTION TO GENERATION XTREME

"...and there arose another generation after them
who did not know the Lord..." —Judges 2:10.

In this opening section of four chapters, we have some "good news" and some "bad news." To get to the good, we have to take some time and read the bad. The bad consists of spiritual and natural attacks. Attacks of a sadistic enemy we know as Satan who hates the purposes of God (destined for our current generation) as accomplished at the cross of Jesus Christ. So this chapter will focus on the "bad news." The good is that God will yet be even greater glorified in reaping the harvest of the righteous among a generation that many have written off.

Perhaps the greatest attack on this current generation is the stigma attached to it. The stigma which says we are useless and have no particular purpose. In one sense, the attack on our generation to cause us to believe that we have no purpose is not new. The above scripture points to a similar generation as ours today. They are perhaps some of the most startling words in the scriptures. They are haunting. They echo down through the corridors of time and drive home to our hearts and ears a truth: that it is possible for an entire generation to arise who 'know not the Lord'.

In it's simplest meaning, the text is a citation of the rebellion of an entire generation of Israelites, those who had descended from the loins of the men whom God had chosen to reveal Himself in glory and power in the exodus from Egypt and the days in the wilderness. These were the men and women who had experienced first-hand both the goodness and severity of the Lord. They had followed the godly leadership through Moses, and later Joshua, and were a part of His covenanted people whom He had chosen.

A part of me cries and mourns in agony over these people, who had experienced the One, True God, and yet had forsaken Him knowingly and deliberately. Another part of me bleeds with compassion, for except the Lord would have mercy on us, who among us could follow Him? Are we not the blind, the deaf, and in need of Him to initiate, to break in on our established, organized disorder we call our existence, to reveal to us the truth, and empower us to live it? However, there is a responsibility to the revelation which God brings. Although Israel was warned, they willingly disobeyed, and their children grew up with no moral guidelines, no restraint on wickedness, and no sense of destiny. Joshua, who had been mentored by Moses and trained and released in the ways of God, never took the time to mentor his replacement. There is no record of the leadership of his day teaching and imparting truth to the next generation. And so the book of Judges opens with those tragic words, *"...and there arose another generation after them who did not know the Lord."*

GENERATION TO GENERATION

So what can we make of this, that will apply to our day and generation? Perhaps if we examine together the truth of this passage of scripture from the Old Testament in the context of the current

WE HAVE LOST OUR HERITAGE AND GROWN COLD AND INDIFFERENT IN THE THINGS OF GOD

world around us, then we can draw a parallel. Hemmingway, who wrote in the nineteen-fifties against the backdrop of a time when religion was becoming irrelevant, introduced the concept in his novel, <u>The Sun Also Rises</u> that society continues to ebb and flow in time as waters upon the seashore. He quoted the immortal book of Ecclesiastes which reminds us that with the rising and setting of the sun all continues just as it was, and "there is no new thing under the sun."

In the first section of the book, we want to set forth an intermingling of both the natural and spiritual causes of the issue at hand. I just mentioned that in one sense the attack of the enemy on our generation is not unique, that it happened in the days following Moses and Joshua; now let me spend a few pages from history to explain the opposite: that he knows by God's design that our generation **is unique** in the timetable of God's purpose and perhaps the final generation to usher in the return of Christ.

The issue is this: the generation that the world and the enemy has termed, "X" is the generation which will surpass the previous generation in extreme passion for Christ and carrying the gospel forward. In the generation spoken of above, Satan had all but destroyed the witness of faith in God through man's free-will choices of idolatry. And according to Ecclesiastes, as Hemmingway discovered, there is no new thing, that is, in context, the battle between flesh and spirit, light and darkness, continues in our generation just as it had in the previous ones. However, there is a difference in our generation that has only occurred in a few others in history and the difference is this: the enemy knows the destiny of this special generation, and is out to destroy it. This is quite a statement. Yet I believe the following chapters will substantiate it. We'll be looking at both spiritual and natural causes.

Let's begin with some visionary thoughts with spiritual roots. The business of destroying an entire generation, whose call and purpose are special in the eternal plans of God, is not a new thing. Indeed, as we shall learn next, it's been tried before.

If we were to look in a general way at the Old Testament, we could say that in essence, it is one great series of battles, where Satan, our enemy, is doing all he can to destroy that which is revealed by God and somehow stop the promised "Seed of Woman" from coming into the earth and destroying him and his works.

Back in Genesis 3, Satan successfully gained entrance and authority into the affairs of mankind by deceiving Eve and causing the fall of man in Adam and Eve's disobedience. Afterwards, he was prophetically given his sentence from the great Judge of all the earth. Somewhere, at some time, there was coming forth, born of woman, a promised seed who would "crush his head" Genesis 3:15.

So the Old Testament brings to us the warfare of souls, and the attempted destruction of the line of David from which the Promise was to come. See the children of Israel, sold into bondage of slavery in Egypt; yet God sent Moses and Joshua to deliver them. See the descendants of Abraham, Isaac, and Jacob, choosing time and time again over one thousand years, to disobey the commands of God, eventually to be sold into

THE RESULT OF ONE SEEMINGLY INSIGNIFICANT EVENT COULD CHANGE THE RESULTING HISTORY FOR ALL TIME

Babylonian captivity; yet God in His mercy spares a remnant and they return to Jerusalem. See the silence of God for four hundred years between the testaments, where all of a sudden God begins to move again when the Jews are the subjects of scorn in the Roman Empire. He sends Jesus to the earth, and a mighty man named John the Baptist heralds His arrival. You need only read the genealogy of Jesus found in Matthew chapter 1 or Luke chapter 3 and study the history of each of the men listed there to see the awesome struggle of Satan's attempt to kill and destroy the seed of woman, and attempt to stop his own eventual downfall.

Out of all of Satan's destructive aims against the human race, God's word highlights two occasions of incredible spiritual warfare over a generation of young people.

Here is a new term for your vocabulary: nexus point. A nexus point is a term that modern-day science has attributed to a turning point in history: like a hinge on a door where mankind and her history stands in the balance, a point at which just one seemingly insignificant event could change the resulting history for all time.

We will now focus on three of those nexus points in history where Satan and his demonic forces have felt it necessary to destroy a generation of young people: one from the Old Testament, one from the New, and then the one this book is about: our current generation. We will call them "sagas" in history.

GENERATION DESTRUCTION:
SAGA ONE: 'THE CASTAWAYS'

The first of these hinge-points in dealing with the destruction of an entire generation was during the time of the captivity in Egypt, where the promised seed, who were the generations following the death of their father Joseph, were tormented, afflicted, and by order of Pharaoh, put to death. If you were to pull back the flesh-and-blood curtain and look at it in terms of the realm of the Spirit, it was Satan's attempt to kill the coming deliverer of the children of Israel. He knew there would be a man coming to bring the people out, and he tried to stop it.

Exodus begins with a king who feared the Hebrew people, and desired to put to death any son born.

"Then Pharaoh commanded all his people saying, "Every son who is born you are to cast into the Nile, and every daughter you are to keep alive." Exodus 1:22.

Satan knew from a prophecy that God had given Abraham, in Genesis, that God would somehow deliver His people out of the captivity of Egypt. He also knew that if he could destroy the Hebrews, he could destroy the chance for the one born who would some day destroy him. Out of these "castaways" came forth Moses and Joshua, and deliverance for the people.

GENERATION DESTRUCTION: SAGA TWO:
'THEY WERE NO MORE'

The second of these hinge points of all-out attack on a generation of young occurred at the time of the first-coming of our Lord Jesus Christ. After His humble birth the wise men from the East come to worship Him, and alert Herod to His appearance on the earth. Herod immediately orders the death of all males under the age of two. Matthew's gospel describes the painful event:

"Then when Herod saw that he had been tricked by the magi, he became very enraged, and sent and slew all the male children who were in Bethlehem and in all its environs, from two years old and under, according to the time which he had ascertained from the magi. Then that which was spoken through Jeremiah the prophet was fulfilled, saying, 'A voice was heard in Ramah, weeping and great mourning, Rachel weeping for her children; and she refused to be comforted, because they were no more.'" Matthew 2:16-18.

What bloodshed! What massive spiritual warfare was taking place in the heavenlies over the birth of the promised Savior! Imagine the incredible carnage, the innocent victims slain and buried because of Satan's attempt to destroy the Seed which would soon destroy him. He is crazy - a liar, a thief, and a murderer. And he knows his time is short as a result of his failure to destroy the mighty Lamb some two thousand years ago.

GENERATION DESTRUCTION:
SAGA THREE: 'THE TIME IS RIGHT NOW'

The third saga, or hinge point of history, we will examine for the purposes of this book is the saga of our current generation. Basically from this point forward we are examining closer this whole theme.

We who are young people today are really mixed up. It's not just the external pressures we see in the natural of our culture around us. It goes deeper. It's not even just the internal pressures we experience because of our age. Ephesians 6 chronicles for us the truth that we are in a constant warfare, wrestling not *"against flesh and blood, but against the rulers, against the powers, against the world forces of this darkness, against the spiritual forces of wickedness in the heavenly places." Ephesians 6:12.*

Unseen with natural eyes, yet more real than that which we see in the natural, there is a battle raging right now. Over your home, over your family, over your job, over your school, over your neighborhood, city, region, and nation there is a battle raging. Angels and demons, forces of light and darkness, strongholds of truth and falsehood: these are just a few words to describe it.

The book of Revelation does a great job in pulling together this truth of the spiritual realm and the battle of the ages raging even now: the first half, or chapters 1-11, pictures the struggle on earth and the resulting persecution of the Church by the world. The second half, or chapters 12-22, pulls back the veil and gives us insight into the spiritual realm, and what is taking place there to cause the problems and persecutions of the Church in the world. It shows the struggle of Satan and his helpers vs. the saints and their Champion, Jesus Christ.

The point is: there is a special battle being fought right now as you read these words. It is a battle for an entire generation of millions of young people. The spiritual causes being explained, let's turn our focus for a few pages to some statistics and realities of what has happened in the natural realm the past thirty or forty years to shape our generation.

ALL IS RIGHT IN OUR OWN EYES

Earlier in the chapter we discussed Satan's attack on the young - destroying babies and infants. And when he's not able to wipe out the baby before birth, he goes into action to war against the babies' very life as that baby struggles to grow into a young person and then an adult. We read in Revelation 12 symbolically of how the great red dragon stands ready to devour the child, the child destined to rule all the nations with a rod of iron. The child is caught up to God and to His throne and soon after, a war in the heavenly realm takes place. The red dragon is thrown down into the earth, along with his followers, and proceeds to spend his time making war with the relatives of the baby who,

NEVER IN THE HISTORY OF MANKIND HAS A GENERATION FALLEN SO HARD, SO FAST

"keep the commandments of God and hold to the testimony of Jesus."
Revelation 12:17.

That Child is Jesus Himself, the red dragon is Satan, and the offspring of the woman is the church: us. If abortion can't kill the promise, then the flood of satanic influences upon the culture can assist in doing it. Never in the history of mankind has a generation of youth fallen so hard, so fast.

I remember when I was a kid attending the public schools. We didn't have any signs up on the walls declaring: "Don't do Drugs," "Just Say No," "Don't Smoke," "Practice Safe Sex," or any such material. My classmates and I were pretty harmless in the mid-seventies in our sheltered suburbian America. The worst shock I ever had was in the sixth grade when I espied a female, rebellious classmate smoking a cigarette after class one day. Other than this, I lived in a rather sheltered condition. Boys would smoke, of course, but a girl smoking was true rebellion!

Although around me things began to change. A whole new concept came to our elementary school when I was entering the sixth grade. The concept was "latch-key kids". It was sort-of an early form of daycare for young mothers who were poor and had to work. When I, at the age of twelve, had both a loving mother and father to go home to, these young kids, at ages two and three, had only a poor, single mom to go home to. In fact statistics show that between 1965 and 1977, the divorce rate doubled. More than 40% of today's young adults had spent time in a single-parent home by age sixteen.[22]

My parents taught me basic moral values, based on the Holy Scriptures and values that their generation had taught them, which I adhered to and still do: stay pure for marriage, don't participate in drugs or alcohol, tell the truth, treat others with respect, pray, and believe in yourself. Yet these basic moral teachings were slowly disappearing from homes and schools all over the country even as they were being taught to me.

I still remember a time in my fifth-grade public school classroom at Hopi Elementary School in Scottsdale, Arizona. The year was 1980, and my teacher was a deep, special woman, who had us all proclaim, "I pledge allegiance to the flag" each morning and then bow our heads for a moment of silent prayer before classes started. But those times soon vanished at the turning of the tide of new legislature which banned prayer in schools in any fashion as initiated by the instructor.

Soon came the concepts of video arcades and home video games, VCRs, M-TV, home video rentals, punk and acid rock music, and later rap, drug deals at school, increased teen violence, teen pregnancy, and AIDS. There were no "AIDS awareness" teachings or programs before I had reached my junior year of high school in 1986. It was just becoming known then and caused a great deal of fear. The concept of the 'gang' began to replace the family unit as the place of formation of young people. Gay/lesbian and women's rights began to come into play in wider extent around the nation. Other forces which shaped our generation were: homelessness, downsizing and corporate layoffs, soaring national debt, the Iran-Contra scandal, the Challenger explosion, fear of holes in the ozone layer, fear of bankrupt social security, and faces of missing children on milk cartons.

Within my twelve years of basic education, from about the mid-seventies until the late eighties, it seemed the whole world had been turned upside down, and reality was changing by the hour. We were slipping silently away as a generation.

I lived and grew in a time of innocence. Now that time is gone.

THE END OF THE INNOCENCE

When I was in the tenth grade our family uprooted and moved away from the home we had been in for almost five years to a mid-size town in north-central Minnesota.

It was a new environment for me. There would be new friends to make, new teachers, new subjects. Throughout my school years, I found it difficult to make new friends, and this was no exception. For several months I didn't meet anybody to really "hang out" with. Then one day, Brian Dufour and I crossed paths. We were the same age and shared similar interests. Once I played a song on our high school radio program for him and his girlfriend, and soon we became friends. Somehow he found all my silly jokes quite humorous. He had a laugh and a smile a mile wide that none could forget. He was a great kid.

After school was out that year we had more time to hang out. He took me golfing, and oh! I was a terrible golfer! But he hung in there with me. Then there was the dreaded driver's test. My sixteenth birthday was approaching, and we would spend much time on the phone together, as he had just gotten his driver's license and he was giving me all of the tips I'd need to get mine.

Late that summer, our family had to move back to Minneapolis because our house wasn't selling. We had to live in it until it was sold, so Brian and I parted ways. Half-way through that year, I lost touch with him and most of the other students up there. One day I came home from school, and my mom announced that one of my classmates had committed suicide.

"Do you know their name?"

"No. I just heard that one of the juniors committed suicide. It was a young man."

Several weeks passed, and I still remember the moment that I heard the news. It was my friend Brian. He had committed suicide.

Apparently he and his girlfriend had been having problems, and also he and his brother. One morning, trying to patch things up, in a desperate attempt he went to her house. There was an argument, and he walked out into his car and shot himself through the skull. That was the end of Brian Dufour.

And that was the end of my innocence. Death was staring me in the face. The Bible tells us that *"the last enemy to be abolished is death"* (I Corinthians 15:26). It had taken away my friend Brian, never to return him again. Death is real. It is cold and hard and real. And: it doesn't play fair.

Or should I say that Satan doesn't play fair? This is the truth - and I urge you to wake up to it - the enemy is after your life - he's after you and he's after me.

This point was made real to me by an incident that happened on a recent ministry trip to Orlando, Florida. I had just finished preaching at a meeting, and was tired and hungry. The facilities were rented and had to be cleaned up before we left. I got impatient and anxious. I guess my humanity was getting the best of me.

Finally, after what seemed like an endless delay, we left the building. Just outside, we were delayed five more minutes by the pastor speaking to somebody. As we got into the van and were headed down the interstate, we had to slow down because of an accident by the side of the road. Apparently, the accident had just happened, and only one police car was there. The ambulance was on its way but hadn't yet arrived. As we slowed down, I was the only one in our van to get a real good look at the accident site. A small car stood smashed in the front, with the windshield blown apart.

It must have been a head-on collision. I'll never forget what my eyes beheld next. In front of the smashed-up vehicle lay the body of a young woman. Blood streamed on the ground, matching the color of her red-checkered dress. The top half of her was covered only by a blanket. She was dead. Killed instantly being thrown through the windshield of her car.

A shudder went right through me as we passed by on into the night. Sometime during that fateful night, an officer would be visiting the home of that young woman and informing her parents of the tragedy. For her, life had come to a sudden halt. No longer would she be around to experience life. Hers had ended, like a match being suddenly blown out. The pastor asked what I had seen. The image of her body flashed vividly in my mind. I couldn't speak. Just then the thought struck.

What if our van hadn't been delayed those five minutes?

The accident had only just taken place; perhaps it was an attack and was meant for us? Perhaps Satan was out to kill us, and it could have been our van laying smashed on the side of the road.

I didn't sleep well that night, as I thought about it. It was another end of my innocence. The reality of life and death had struck home again, and I would never be the same. There are many in our generation who have only felt the hopelessness but never the loving arms of a tender Savior; who have been killed in accidents or other ways without hope.

On December 7, 1941, there was peace and quiet surrounding the US Naval Base in Hawaii. When suddenly, early in the morning, there appeared a massive radar blip on the screen. Hundreds of planes from the Japanese armed forces swooped over at breakneck speed, opening fire and dropping a barrage of bombs, killing and wounding many soldiers and causing America to enter the war to end all wars.

I recently heard a radio broadcast which declared, "This fateful day marked for America the end of her age of innocence..." And this is where we are today.

Yes, Satan is after you and me. But let's take it a step further: he's after our entire generation.

CULTURAL BACKDROP OF OUR AGE: THERE IS NO KING IN ISRAEL

Let's travel back in a time machine for just a moment to get an over-arching view which will help us in the discovery of the roots and causes of life in our generation. It is interesting to trace the history of intellectual thought over the past five hundred years. As a people who used to be shaped by the Bible, we have taken some serious downward spirals. Most scholars of history can agree upon three phases of change of thought which have affected us in our current generation.

First, the late medieval era, from about 1000 A.D. to 1530 A.D. This is termed, "Theonomous" meaning, "the law of God." Basically, the desire for the will of God to be accomplished influenced much of society, government, and family life. Culture in the West was shaped by language which emphasized God and put His law and will at the center of existence. Next came what is known as the, "modern era," from about 1530 A.D. to 1885 A.D. This is termed, "Autonomous" meaning, "the law of the self." Basically, every-

THE CRY OF MANY DEEP INSIDE IS, "WHO AM I?"

thing in culture began to shift until the attitude of life centered around the theme, "what does this have to do with me?" The law of a particular group became most important....the "me, myself, and I" attitude prevailed in shaping society. The third era, of which we find ourselves in now, is termed the, "post-modern era," dating from about 1885 A.D. to the present day. It can be termed, "Anomos" meaning, "without law," a world without law, kind of like the scripture reference we began this section with, *"in those days there was no king in Israel, and there arose a people who knew not the Lord."* People in our generation as a whole, and especially young adults, don't know who they are. Diversity is the accepted norm and there are no absolutes or standards by which to base one's own existence. The cry of many deep inside is, "who am I?"

Our world has grown up with many a tare sown among the wheat, many a truth mixed with a half-truth, and many a compromise with the world and how the culture around us thinks and acts. In short, we have been left with a generation of no moral absolutes, one which preaches its own gospel that whatever philosophical brand of belief you subscribe to becomes your salvation. Our educational system has become one which has left God out of the equation and stresses individualism and selfishness. Hemmingway's conclusion left him to live a life of continual compromise of moral standards, and then to die in alcoholism and sheer loneliness.

Life has become filled with self, and selfishness runs rampant. Not that it always hasn't, but the Apostle Paul, writing to Timothy, gives us a picture of a re-focusing of love in the end times. Count the number of times the word love is used in this passage and the way in which it is used: *"But realize this, that in the last days difficult times will come. For men will be <u>lovers</u> of self, <u>lovers</u> of money, boastful, arrogant, revilers, disobedient to parents, ungrateful, unholy, <u>unloving</u>, irreconcilable, malicious gossips, without self-control, brutal, <u>haters</u> of good, treacherous, reckless, conceited, <u>lovers</u> of pleasure rather than <u>lovers</u> of God..."* 2 Timothy 3:1-4. There are five indictments on man in the end times listed in this scripture: lovers of self, lovers of money, unloving, haters of good (lovers of wickedness), and lovers of pleasure. To sum up the thought, the focus is on the love of everything it seems except God. RATHER THAN "lovers of God, men become, "lovers of self," like a universal tea party:

"I had a little tea party,
One afternoon at three;
'Twas very small, three guests in all,
Just I, myself, and me.
Myself ate up the sandwiches,
While I drank up the tea,
'Twas also I who ate the pie
And passed the cake to me."

—*anonymos*

A FIELD WITH NO BOUNDARIES

On the natural side of things, Satan has done an effective job in labeling our generation. Douglas Copeland coined the term, "Generation X" in his book by the same name in 1991. It is a tale of languid youths musing over "mental ground zero – the location where one visualizes oneself if an atomic bomb was dropped." He capsulated our generation with the stigmata of hopelessness. What he failed to realize in his secular book was that there are spiritual causes and effects of sin and lawlessness in the culture which have created the monster. On a recent Voice of America broadcast in Europe it was reported that the X'rs are "lazy, they watch too much TV, they're overwhelmed from the demands of life, their standard of living is lower than their parents, and they have no identity."[23]

Ron Hutchcraft, who travels the country holding seminars on relating the gospel to culture and making it relevant, recently shared in a conference that in today's world, people are "playing on a field with no boundaries. There is no sense of violation." And because our gospel no longer cuts to the hearts of our hearers, the individual sees no relevance for Christ...a savior is not needed if you've nothing to be saved from.

According to a book by George Barna, "Generation X can be described as being: 1. serious about life because they have been exposed to too much too early, 2. stressed out due to all the fast moving changes in the world, 3. self-reliant due to so many of the institutions of the world that have let them down, including family and government, 4. highly "spiritual" because they have drawn the conclusion that there must be more to life than the natural things, so they are open to the supernatural realm, and, 5. survivors, in other words, able to accept what is while longing for more."[24]

"We are handicapped and unable to bring about the changes that are longed for," writes David Plaistad, "We see the need but are unable to prescribe the cure. Though many are not able to identify why they are struggling we are aware that we are missing something. We long for intimacy in relationship but find ourselves too afraid of being vulnerable. The result is that we fail at maintaining any relationship of depth."[25]

Statistics gathered in research in the mid-nineties from Glen Charles, a director of a Youth With A Mission base in Wisconsin, reveal more truth about our generation. "In the 1990's," Glen writes, "70-80% of teenagers are sexually active, and the average young person spends eighty hours each week listening to rock and roll or watching M-TV. In the 1950's, the authority structure for the youth was ranked in this manner:

> 1. Church
> 2. Government
> 3. Parents
> 4. School
> 5. Friends

In the 1970's, when I was growing up, church authority dropped to 3. Now in the 1990's and beyond, here are the statistics,

1. Peers
2. School
3. Media
4. Parents
5. Government"[26]

Does this sound the least bit shocking? Because of the break-down of the family structure, the complacency and spreading liberality of the church, and the drive of the media, the authority which is supposed to be respected and followed in the family unit and in the government is lacking. Roles have been completely and utterly reversed. We now are living in a generation where "anything goes" as in the days of Judges, *"There was no king in Israel, and each man did that which was right in his own eyes"* Judges 2:10.

Peers have replaced the Church as the place where morals and character and respect for authority is formed. One example of this is the concept of gangs, who have sprung up in the poor, inner-city regions because of the breakdown of the family. According to Carroll Thompson, teacher at Christ For The Nations in Dallas, Texas, there are three basic life-structures of support by which we are given peace: the family unit, the church, and the society we live in (or government). A break-down in any of these areas causes a crack in the individual, and he/she must find another avenue for the formation of their life. In a following chapter of this book we will discuss the implications of the "fatherless generation" which we have around us and God's mighty counterpart in becoming a Father to all who would call upon Him through relationship with His Son.

In general, there is widespread rebellion against authority. In one sense, there is nothing new here; ever since the fateful day, documented in Genesis 4:9, when wicked Cain rose up and slew righteous Abel, we have seen rebellion in the earth. Indeed, the "mark of Cain" exists everywhere, as men and women roam about the earth, driven from the presence of their Creator, ask-ing the question, "Am I my brother's keeper?" The resounding answer from society is "No!" The resounding answer from Almighty God is "Yes!"

"...just as they did not see fit to acknowledge God any longer, God gave them over to a depraved mind, to do those things which are not proper, being filled with all unrighteousness, wickedness, greed, evil; full of envy, murder, strife, deceit, malice; they are gossips, slanderers, haters of God, insolent, arrogant, boastful, inventors of evil, disobedient to parents, without understanding, untrustworthy, unloving, unmerciful; and, although they know the ordinance of God, that those who practice such things are worthy of death, they not only do the same, but also give hearty approval to those who practice them." Romans 1:28-32.

Quite a list, yet the same conditions exist today as when Paul composed his epistle to the church at Rome.

If you want to hear the heartbeat of a generation, just listen to its music. Music is an expression of the soul. Just listen to the secular lyrics sung through the fleshly prophets of our genera-tion, which speak of hopelessness, death, relational problems, family breakdowns. Much of the rap coming out right now is sensual, devilish, and filled with a poor choice of vocabulary.

Curt Cobane, a rock-star/drug-addict who sang the blues of this generation in his haunting parables of a lost world, recently committed suicide, and half-a-million disillusioned teenagers gathered at his estate and stayed there three days during his funeral and burial.

If you desire to see the rebellion, just look at the graffiti which surrounds you. It has taken over the inner cities like a plague.

I will say it again: there has thus arisen a generation of wander-ers. On a recent ministry trek across Western Europe, I noticed them everywhere I went. On the trains, the ships, the busses, the subways, the street corners were young people, traveling about, perhaps "in search of themselves." Many wearing backpacks, and those whom I spoke with, lost.

In his book, <u>Between Two Worlds</u>, preacher John R.W. Stott gives a startling continuance of this truth:

"Seldom if ever in its long history has the world witnessed such a self-conscious revolt against authority...What seems new today, however, is both the world-wide scale of the revolt and the philosophical arguments with which it is sometimes buttressed. There can be no doubt that the twentieth century has been caught up in a global revolution, epitomized in the two World Wars. The old order is giving place to anew. All the accepted authorities (family, school, university, State, Church, Bible, Pope, God) are being challenged. Anything which savors of 'establishment', that is, of entrenched privilege or unassailable power, is being scrutinized and opposed...

> In economics it (this generation) protests against the exploitation of the poor and against the new social servitude, slavery to the consumer market and to the machine. In industry it (this generation) protests against the class confrontation between management and unions, and calls for a greater measure of responsible participation for the workers. In education it (this generation) protests against indoctrination, the misuse of the classroom to bend the malleable minds of the young into predetermined shapes, and calls instead for young people to develop their own personal potential."[27]

It was said of Cain, who rejected brotherhood within his own family by slaying Abel, *"You shall be a vagrant and a wanderer on the earth."* Genesis 4:12.

So goes the cycle. Separated from God, pronounced guilty in the judgment of God against them, sentenced thus to wander in search of truth and always to come up empty are our own youth. What then is the third of these points in history? Could it be perhaps that you and I are living in it right now? Is this the time of the end, where Satan is using all his tactics in order to destroy a generation? If so, why? Let's examine even deeper the downfall of these past twenty or so years and see if we can find an answer.

CHAPTER TWO

HARVESTING THE FIELDS OF THE FATHERLESS

"Remove not the ancient landmark, which thy fathers have set..." Proverbs
22:28 *KJV*

"And they will be mine," says the Lord of hosts, "on the day that I
prepare my own possession, and I will have compassion on them as a man
spares his own son who serves him." Malachi 3:17.

"The strength of a nation lies in the homes of its people."
—Abraham Lincoln

In the following chapter the theme of the fatherless, relation-
ship-less generation will be more fully developed. We are a
generation of fatherless sons and daughters. Tips will also be
given for the Moses' out there who desire to spend their energy
in building relationships with our culture and harvest the fields
of the fatherless. Finally, we'll look God's way of redeeming the
fatherless generation through raising up vision to grab ahold of
the previous generation's anointing and bring it into the present
with a new expression, as well as the scriptural warrant in these
days for the Moses' and Joshua's to join hand in hand and work

together toward the common cause of Christ and advancing his Kingdom. First, let's look at the hopelessness of the fatherless and the hope of the Father in response to it.

You may remember in the previous chapter as well as in the introduction we were discussing the breakdown of society in three levels: the home, the church, and the civil government. Without these basic support systems, our lives become disillusioned, disengaged, and disassociated.

We're looking here at the breakdown of fathers in the lost generation. Godly character is formed within the structure of the

ASK FOR THE ANCIENT PATHS

home. A son or daughter needs tender love, which exercises itself with acceptance, lovingkindness, and tough love, which exercises itself with discipline and authority. The authority of the father is needed combined with the nurturing of the mother to form a young life in righteousness. Jack Levine, executive director of the Florida Center for Children and Youth recently wrote in the newspaper, "We're about to lose a generation." He listed the fatherless aspect as high on the list as to the reasoning behind his shocking statement.

One old story tells the tale of two young brothers who were carpenters returning for a visit to the home they grew up in. One of the brothers was soon to be married and the old house was to be torn down and a new one erected on its site. For years neither of the brothers had visited the cottage, as it had been leased.

As they entered now and started the work of demolishing the place, again and again floods of tender memories swept over them. By the time they reached the kitchen they were well-nigh overcome with their emotions. There was the place where the old kitchen table had stood, with the family Bible, where they had knelt every evening. They were recalling now with a pang how in later years they had felt a little superior to that time-honored custom carefully observed by their father.

Said one, "We're better off that he was, but we're not better men."

The other seemed to agree, replying, "I'm going back to the church and the old ways of following the Lord, and in my new home I am going to make room for worship as Dad did."

"Thus says the Lord, 'Stand by the ways and see and ask for the ancient paths, where the good way is, and walk in it; and you shall find rest for your souls." Jeremiah 6:16.

These two brothers chose to return to the "good way," but unfortunately, the choices of our past generations leave a testimony against us, and many sons don't choose the "good way," for the Lord continues with this phrase,

"But they said, 'We will not walk in it.'" Jeremiah 6:16.

So perhaps this true story is one of bygone days. For even though the above story has a happy ending and followed the first part of the scripture from Jeremiah, sadly, with the breakdown of the family, our current generation does not end so happily, as it follows the second part of that scripture. Our generation has said, "We will not walk in it."

You see, there is no guarantee that just because our fathers walked in the ways of the Lord, that we will do the same. Billy

Graham has jokingly said in his evangelistic crusades, "Just because you are born in a garage doesn't make you a car." There is no guarantee of your sons and daughters following God just because you did. And the mistakes of fatherhood and mother-hood can make their mark on the next generation. One only has to read the unfortunate story of righteous Eli and his unrighteous sons in I Samuel 2: 12-17. His sons are described as, "worthless men" who "did not know the Lord." Eli was a good man, but he failed in disciplining his children, and as a result they had no respect for him. The problem is not with the children themselves, but with the lack of godly influences. For many, the Boomer/Buster generation let them down; they divorced at an unprecedented rate.

"I hate to say this, but we've nearly lost a generation," says Pastor Bob Ware, member of the Orange County Citizen's Commission for Children. "The children we're talking about are children who are born to families with no male influence and no money. They may not have the capacity to deeply love. We've got a generation of children who don't know how to bond or how to love. These kids grow up angry and deprived. If we don't turn it around, the system as we know it will collapse."

Let us look at the loss of the men of standard and the effects upon "Generation X."

WILL THE REAL DAD PLEASE STAND UP?

"I don't have a dad and I miss it. I don't have a big brother. Sometimes I get real lonely." —Matthew, age 8

Matthew is the son of a young single mother living in Orlando, Florida. He's just one of the current statistics. Just thirty years ago, one in forty children was born to an unwed mother; today the statistic is one in five. Over one million teenage girls become pregnant each year, and about half give birth.

In a recent article on the welfare system, The New York Times quoted one 32-year-old Baltimore man who had fathered six children with four women—none of whom he married or promised long-term assistance. At one point, three women were pregnant with his children at the same time.

His explanation: "I was wild, like all kids."

Can you see the breakdown in the morals? One of the ways to pawn off the guilt we feel as the consequences of our actions is to blame another, and rightly so, we are examining a lack of fatherhood one of the causes of our lost generation. This man was a bastard son raising bastard children. Chances are, this man never bonded with a father in his own life.

There's a Spanish story of a father and son who had become estranged. The son ran away, and the father set off to find him. He searched for months to no avail. Finally, in a last desperate effort to find him, the father put an ad in a Madrid newspaper. The ad read:

"Dear Paco, meet me in front of this newspaper office at noon on Saturday. All is forgiven. I love you. Your Father."

On Saturday, eight hundred Pacos showed up, looking for forgiveness and love from their fathers.

Recently I heard the true story on the radio of a man in a Federal penitentiary who came up with the great idea of creating Valentine's Day cards for the men to give to their fathers. He set out immediately in his creative mode, designing and printing beautiful cards for the coming holiday.

He put an ad four weeks previous to the event on the bulletin board, selling the cards for $1 each. Sadly, no one responded. Three weeks before the day he dropped his price to $.75. No response. A week later he dropped the price to $.50. Still no one responded. In a last-ditch effort to at least recoup his

OF THE 5,000 MEN IN THE PRISON, NOT ONE HAD A FATHER IN THE HOME WHILE THEY WERE GROWING UP

money, he dropped the price to $.25 one week before the day, and still, no one responded.

When he finally gave in and offered them for free and still had no response, he went to the warden. He was shocked at the news. Of the 5,000 men in the prison, not one had a father in the home while they were growing up.

And I suppose this kind of thing has been happening, to some extent, in every generation. Even the Psalmist wrote, *"For my father and my mother have forsaken me, but the Lord will take me up."* Psalm 27:10.

SAY IT LOUD, SAY IT CLEAR

As far as young women go, problems take on similar fashion. I have ministered to several young women who were experiencing all sorts of problems with male authority. Of the multitudes of young women out there, many are caught in the web of addiction, others with immoral actions and lifestyles, and many of them have never bonded their fathers in harmonious love and recognition of godly authority. As we've already explained, much of the cause of the breakdown has been a lack of strong fatherhood.

So be we young men or women, we have a difficult time in relationships. We're especially weakened when it comes to opening up our hearts. Because we haven't received love or value, it is hard to give it.

The lyrics to a pop song ring with words of truth:

"Every generation blames the one before.
And all of their frustrations come beating on your door.
I know that I'm a prisoner to all my father held so dear,
I know that I'm a hostage, to all his hopes and fears,
I just wish I could have told him in the living years.
Say it loud, say it clear. You can listen as well as you hear.
It's too late when we die, to admit we don't see eye to eye.

I wasn't there that morning, when my father passed away,
I didn't get to tell him, all the things I had to say.
I think I caught his spirit, later that same year.
I'm sure I heard his echo in my baby's newborn tears.
I just wish I could have told him in the living years."[31]

This song expresses the pain of unresolved childhood conflict. Like many others, these lyrics reveal to us something of the cry of this generation.

What happens when a father doesn't relate in a godly way to his son or daughter? In the above song, the unresolved conflict caused remorse instead of there being a release for the next generation to become all they can with encouragement.

In Ireland, for example, at least in the South, it is for the most part the women who are and were raising the children. For many generations the men would spend their time working, or just plain being lazy, come home to eat, and then spend their evenings at the local pubs drinking. Alcoholism goes back many generations, so for generations it is the women who have been forced into doing much of the work of raising the children, while the men take a back seat in the home. Many of the fathers either don't realize the importance of their place, or refuse and rebel against it. The men aren't rising up and being men or fathers.

AN EXPERIMENT OF EXPERIENCE

Let's personalize this with a miniature experiment. This is aimed at Gen. X'ers, though whatever age you are you can participate.

Here are two questions for you to personally answer right now; the answers are private and meant to be between you and the Lord. Grab a pen or a pencil. Ready?

Question One: "How do you look at yourself as an individual?"

Question Two: "How do you relate to God?"

Take a moment and answer each of the two questions. Don't hurry your answers. Now assuming you've got an answer to each of them, let's see what those answers reveal. The answer to the first question reveals your formation in character. How well your parent/s or peers raised you and allowed a godly formation to take place in your character. The answer to the second reveals your relationship to your earthly father, and thus possibly to your Heavenly Father. Because God ordained the father in the home to mirror His own likeness, the way in which you relate to God is the way in which you have been brought up to relate to your earthly dad. Maybe you feel your answers are great, or maybe they could be better. Remember, it is only a little experiment. And whatever your past experience has been in your growth and formation in Jesus Christ, your present and future experience can and will change.

THE FATHER GOD ORDAINED IN THE HOME TO MIRROR HIS OWN LIKENESS

I believe we have a generation where in the area of the lack of fatherhood, and consequent hardship in relationships, much change is going to be forged by those who can cast away the fear of rejection and begin to reach out to others. "Searching hearts are more open to truth than satisfied hearts," writes X'er David Plaistad, "God has given my generation a hungry heart. The down side is that we tend to be consumers, even with the gospel of Christ. The upside is that we are hungry to find something real from our God. We want real relationship. We want real spiritual healing. We want real revival. We want real power and influence in order to bring change to the world that we have judged as near meaningless. We are looking for a real God with real goods."[32]

THE COMPELLING CALL: A WORD TO THE MOSES GENERATION

Let's look a little closer at the story Jesus told of the prodigal son. The difference in this kid is not a lack of fatherhood, but simply of rebellion. He runs away from the comfort and security of the home and indulges in sensual pleasures, until he finds living with the pigs is not so desirous after all. Then he decided to return to his father.

"But while he was still a long way off, his father saw him, and felt compassion for him, and ran and embraced him, and kissed him....And he said to him, 'My child, you have always been with me, and all that is mine is yours. But we had to be merry and rejoice, for this brother of your was dead and has begun to live, and was lost and has been found." Lk. 15:21, 31-32.

This is also a prophetic picture of the transformation of the end times. The lost and wayward sons, those who have rebelled since birth against their heavenly Father, will return, and He will gather them in His bosom; yet so it shall be with you who are young men/women and fathers/mothers in the faith. You will need the same compassion and tenderness to minister to and accept the multitudes who will be drawn into the Kingdom through the Father's love and the Father's power poured forth through you.

In our day, God is calling many a Moses to begin to reach out in various ways to relate to the younger generation. Love and acceptance will speak to us in ways that church structure never could. Strong truth in action is a part of this kind of love. Acceptance for who we are as a generation and who we are as individuals can be a big step in the right direction. The father in the story didn't judge his son, he just accepted him for who he was and embraced him.

Did you ever stop to think that of all the thousands of disciples who followed Jesus those three years, yet He only "called" twelve of them? The rest were **compelled** to follow Him; they were drawn by the compassion and love which flowed out from Him. It will be the same way in the end days. Many will be compelled to ask you of what spirit you possess. Many will be compelled to follow Christ because He is so real within you. Moses is called to train and impart vision, and Joshua is called to possess the land. Both groups will be filled with such passion for Jesus that the lost and wayward sons and daughters will be drawn to a relationship with God.

THE MARKS OF A SPIRITUAL MOSES

A few years ago I heard a sermon preached by Pastor Terry Christ on the "Marks of a Spiritual Father." Let me share his twelve key points with you, along with my comments, directing this at the Moses' out there who have gained a place of experience and maturity. Terry compared spiritual parenting with natural parenting, and although they are not the same thing in the Kingdom, still there are interesting parallels one can draw from each to apply. Many of these points are found in I John as John addressed different believers that he had helped oversee in love and discipline.

First, they assume responsibility for the family. This is the mark of a true father, a true leader. God puts the responsibility for the family on the father. In Acts 20 Paul gives charge to the leadership at the church at Ephesus, and shares with them, *"Be on guard for yourselves and for all the flock, among which the Holy Spirit has made you overseers, to shepherd the church of God which He purchased with His own blood." Acts 20:28.*

Second, they are not reliant upon those around them to determine their course. They are constant and stabilized and build relationships with those who are constant. When I had my first son, I remember the moment I left the hospital with this beautiful six-pound little man in my arms. The hospital and the nurses didn't leave a book on how to raise him! It was my responsibility. I learned hints from good dads around me and sought the Lord on direction, strength, and help.

Third, they are not insecure. Spiritual dads have learned security from the presence of God, and they know who they are in Christ and his truths. Security in oneself brings security to the family. Some leaders who are spiritual fathers have gathered together around them people who are stronger than they are in certain areas, thus offsetting their own weaknesses without feeling the least bit inferior or insecure in doing so. "The first method for estimating the intelligence of a ruler is to look at the men he has around him" said Niccolo Machiavelli.

Fourth, they have a relationship with THE Father as a pattern. Spiritual fathers have spent time and learned over a period of years to get to know intimately the Father of lights, in whom there is no variation or shadow of turning. Each member of the Godhead has a particular voice, personality, and uniqueness. By

EACH MEMBER OF THE GODHEAD HAS A PARTICULAR VOICE, PERSONALITY AND UNIQUENESS

spending time with the Father, He supernaturally imparts His ways. Moses did this. He learned the Father's ways, while the children of Israel only learned His acts. *"He will cry to me, 'Thou art my Father, My God, and the rock of my salvation.'" Psalm 89:26.*

Fifth, they are selfless – willing to lay down their life for the family. Jesus was the original pattern for this kind of selfless life. He was the good shepherd who laid down His life for the sheep. Spiritual fathers are willing to pay a greater price than anyone around them. Perhaps an ultimate price.

Sixth, they are spiritual thinkers and strategists. It takes time to think things through. Fathers take the time necessary to hear the Spirit speaking to them and look at various situations in a different way. Strategies must be developed for children which allow them opportunities to see their own character faults themselves and the means to correct them, as well as room to grow and explore their own gifts. Many sheep in the body are never given an opportunity to grow because their shepherds have not taken the time to pray over them and release them in special strategies for their own growth and growth for the Kingdom.

Seventh, they have a passion for unity. Spiritual dads, since they are secure and strong in themselves and in Christ, can lay down their own particular opinions for the sake of a greater cause of unity. As Dr. Lance Wonders, one of the spiritual fathers in my own life once taught me, "In the essentials, unity. In non-essentials, liberty. In all things, charity." If more leaders would put this statement on their bathroom mirror and live by it, there would be much less in-fighting and more loving in the Body.

Eighth, spiritual fathers understand authority. Back all the way in the garden, God gave man authority over almost all of His created order. All but one thing, that is. Other men. Spiritual fathers recognize they have authority over the flock as a whole, over the family as a whole, but each individual member is answerable only to the Heavenly Father for his/her own sins, redemption, and sanctifying work. The shepherd tends, guards, and prays for his flock, and his individual sheep. That is where a leader's authority begins and ends. Prayer is the ultimate authority as we relinquish our rights to control to God alone and He changes people and leads His flock.

Ninth, they are providers. In that passage from Acts 20 quoted earlier, Paul goes on to say to the Ephesian leadership, *"I have coveted no one's silver or gold or clothes. You yourselves know that these hands have ministered to my own needs and to the men who were with me. In everything I showed you that by working hard in this manner you must help the weak and remember the words of the Lord Jesus, that He Himself said, 'It is more blessed to give than receive.'"* Acts 20:33-35. This is a radical thought in today's selfish church culture. Most leaders expect that their labor for the church should yield them financial blessing. Yet Paul often took a different road. He recognized that tithes and offerings that went to supply his own needs may cause the weak to stumble, so he chose to work with his hands during certain seasons and provide for the needs of himself and his team. A good father is a good spiritual and natural provider.

Tenth, they understand what it means to be a servant. Jesus Himself spoke the memorable words, *"And do not call anyone on earth your father; for One is your Father, He who is in heaven. And do not be called leaders, for One is your Leader, that is, Christ. But the greatest among you shall be your servant." Matthew 23:9-11.*

Eleventh, they speak prophetically, assisting in determining the spiritual destiny of their children. A spiritual father can have not only vision, but an ability to see the potential in someone and develop a strategy to see them brought forth into what they are called to do. Like Jesus' relationship with Simon, whom He prophetically called, "Peter," or, "the rock" long before he was a "rock." He prayed for him before his temptation that though Satan would sift him like wheat he would "not fall." And then later He personally appeared to Him after the resurrection and restored him to strength. On the day of Pentecost "the rock" was seen by all and a changed man stood up and preached Christ.

Twelfth, they speak inspirationally. "You can do it." Spiritual fathers are encouragers and they are patient to wait for the fruit of their labors in their kids. In their hearts, if the ones whom they serve can outdo them and outrun them, they have done their job. Quietly in their heart, with no need for recognition, they can patiently look at those whom they have inspired, who may be far exceeding them in their own ministries, and say, "to God alone the glory." Mark Twain once quipped, "When I was a boy of fourteen, my father was so ignorant I could hardly stand to have the old man around. But when I got to be twenty-one, I was astonished at how much he had learned in seven years."

What about spiritual moms? In a sense, the need in our day for women to take interest in other younger women and younger men around them is just as tantamount as the need for spiritual dads. Many Gen.Xer's have never been fathered or mothered properly. Young daughters of the Almighty, search out older women who can begin to speak and pray into your life. Look around you. If you are a female mentor (a Miriam or a Mary for example), are you seeking the heart of God for the young around you, maybe just two or three younger women, with whom you can initiate relationship and begin to pray for and get to know? Perhaps meet for coffee and share some scriptural truth and valuable life experience with them? Oh, how strong in the heart of God for the generations to work together in community and relationship in this simple yet effective manner! *"Older women likewise are to be reverent in their behavior, not malicious gossips, nor enslaved to much wine, teaching what is good, that they may encourage the young women to love their husbands, to love their children, to be sensible, pure, workers at home, kind, being subject to their own husbands, that the word of God may not be dishonored."* Titus 2:2-5.

A DOUBLE PORTION FOR GENERATION X

All along, we've been examining fathers and sons, those who are called to be the Moses', and those called who are trained to fight and take the promised land. Even though Joshua was not a spring chicken when God called Him to arise after the death of Moses, his generation were all young warriors who stepped out in faith and accomplished the vision of the past generation.

Another scriptural example of this is found in I Kings 18 through II Kings 9 with the stories of Elijah and Elisha. It is a fascinating story to read of how the anointing on the past was conferred to the next generation.

We've spoken up until this point of spiritual roots and causes of where we are now, and of natural factors which have placed such an atmosphere upon an entire generation. However, one

WE NEED TO LEARN TO LOOK AND SEE WHAT THERE WAS IN THE PREVIOUS GENERATION THAT WAS UNIQUE TO THEM

theme I'm introducing here is that we need to learn to look and see what there was in the previous generation that was unique to them, and what there was that can become a part of our current generation and be passed on, like the mantle of authority given to Elisha at the death of Elijah. As the baton from one generation to the next passes, the importance is that the previous generation lets it go, and that the new generation embraces the power and yet finds a new expression of it. For example, Elisha did twice the miracles of Elijah, and he did them differently, under a double portion anointing.

The wisdom now is to get ahold of God for yourself, and if you are an X'er, find out what God is calling you to do, and who He's calling you to be. Let the Holy Spirit spur you forward in your faith to examine the power and calling of the previous generation and then move forward with a double portion of that power, just like Elisha. There is of course a price to pay for this kind of transference, and later in the book we'll be examining further the "how" when we look at instilling various discilplines, the topic of spiritual covering, and mentorship and apprenticeship.

Here we are casting vision for the fields of the fatherless to be transformed into the harvest fields of Father's family. If you are a Moses, the wisdom for you is going to be to transfer only a portion of what you have received to the next generation, and allow them the creativity and open response to accept parts of it and reject parts of it depending on the uniqueness of their calling. Harry S. Truman, when asked about fatherhood, responded, "I have found the best way to give advice to your children is to find out what they want and then advise them to do it." Let's look at two passages of scripture which confirm God's plan to have two generations, old and young, working side by side but with different anointings to get the job done.

HAND IN HAND WITH A SWORD AND A STAFF

"But Peter, taking his stand with the eleven, raised his voice and declared to them, 'And it shall be in the last days,' God says, 'that I will pour forth of My Spirit upon all mankind; and your sons and your daughters shall prophesy, and your young men shall see visions, and your old men shall dream dreams; even upon My bondslaves, both men and women, I will in those days pour forth of My Spirit and they shall prophesy" (Acts 2:14a, 17-18).

Here you can see a tremendous picture for these last days. The old men dream the dreams, and the young men see the visions, and the anointing of the Spirit is upon both equally. When Peter pulled this scripture out of Joel, he maybe didn't realize that it was a powerful confirmation for the Changing of the Guard!

"The death of the dreams of the past generation," says apostolic leader Larry Alberts, "should be the birthing of the next."

The passage in Acts is a clear picture of how the end is supposed to look: God brings the wisdom of the old, and clashes it with the zeal of the young, and both groups work together in unison to do the work of the Lord in the last days. You and me are going to work together.

The prophetical book of Zechariah, chapter 8, gives us a precious peek into the realm of the Spirit and God's hidden plans for His last-days family. It declares,

THE DEATH OF THE DREAMS OF THE PAST GENERATION SHOULD BE THE BIRTHING OF THE NEXT

"Thus says the Lord of Hosts, 'Old men and old women will again sit in the streets of Jerusalem, each man with his staff in his hand because of age. And the streets of the city will be filled with boys and girls playing in its streets."

Do you see the beautiful picture of end-times unity? Jesus prayed in the garden, *"That they may all be one, even as You, Father, are in me, and I in You, that they also may be in Us; that the world may believe that You did send Me." John 17:21.* There is a gem of truth here: the unity coming in the Body will reflect the unity experienced between the three members of the Trinity. Each member of the Trinity flows in unique ministries, and each one builds upon each other, moment by moment, to flow in unity.

The picture of the last of the last days is that of multi-colored, multi-faceted, multi-national, multi-cultural, and varied ages living in harmony as a part of a family of God's making. The wisdom of the old, who carry their staffs, symbolizing both wisdom and authority, merges with the zeal and energy of the young, those "children who play in the streets," and together, they join hands, one holding a staff, the other a sword, and they move the work of God forward. For the purposes of this illustration, the staff symbolizes one "way" to do ministry, and the sword symbolizes another "way" to do it. Both of them are needed, and the anointing is different for one carrying a staff that for one carrying a sword, but each can be united in getting the job done.

I remember reading the whole trilogy of <u>The Lord of the Rings</u> as a fifteen year-old. In one section during the second of the books, <u>The Two Towers</u>, there is a huge battle scene, and old Gandalf with his staff and young Aragorn with his sword fight side by side. Each one has a different style of fighting and each item in their hand accomplishes different things, but each is unique and the one cannot win without the assistance of the other.

Jeremiah saw these days and expressed them as, *"Then the virgin shall rejoice in the dance, and the young men and the old, together, for I will turn their mourning into joy, and will comfort them, and give them joy for their sorrow"* (Jeremiah 31:13).

The young need what the old have built. Joshua needs Moses.

> "An old man, going a lone highway,
> Came at the evening, cold and gray,
> To a chasm, vast and deep and wide,
> Through which was flowing a sullen tide.
> The old man crossed in the twilight dim;
> The sullen stream had no fears for him;
> But he turned when safe on the other side,
> And built a bridge to span the tide.

"Old man," said a fellow pilgrim near,
"You are wasting strength with building here;
Your journey will end with the ending day;
You never again must pass this way;
You have crossed the chasm, deep and wide—
Why build you the bridge at the eventide?"

The builder lifted his old gray head:
"Good friend, in the path I have come," he said,
There follows after me today
A youth whose feet must pass this way.
This chasm that has been naught to me
To that fair-haired youth may a pitfall be.
He, too, must cross in the twilight dim;
Good friend, I am building the bridge for him."

—anonymous.

"We are like dwarfs," wrote the monk Bernard of Chartres. "Seated on the shoulders of giants. We see more things than the ancients and things more distant, but it is due neither to the sharpness of our sight nor the greatness of our stature. It is simply because they have lent us their own."

In the same way, the old need what the young are building. Moses needs Joshua.

One example from church history is from the England of the 1600's. Even then, the Holy Spirit was revealing to the young something of the power of the previous generations and challenging some to walk in it, but with an increase. George Fox, founder of the Quakers, saw this. As a young man of twenty, he went out in the fields surrounding his home and sought God with all his heart. As a result, God poured out an unusually strong measure of anointing on his life and he began not only to preach but to move in strong discernment and even in signs and wonders. The older generation of leadership needed this fresh input that was placed upon him for adding to their ministry, for they had a strong power to preach but the power of the spirit didn't permeate their lives like it did in young George's. Just one example of this is drawn from his journal. He began to walk in continual discernment of people around him, so much so that the older leaders were amazed.

"As I was walking," wrote Fox in 1652 in England, "I heard old people and workpeople to say, 'Here is such a man as never was, he knows people's thoughts...several people came also and I discerned their conditions...and the mighty power of the Lord was so over all that the priest Bennet spoke to me and asked me if I had the spirit of discerning, I told him I had, which made him to tremble."[33]

As we have already pointed out in earlier chapters, there is a unique calling in this very hour, lasting perhaps an entire gener-

> THERE IS A UNIQUE CALLING IN THIS VERY HOUR, LASTING PERHAPS AN ENTIRE GENERATION OF 40 YEARS, FOR AN EXPRESSION OF CHRISTIANITY TO BURST FORTH WHICH IS SPECIAL FOR OUR TIMES.

ation of 40 years, for an expression of Christianity to burst forth which is special for our times. And this expression encompasses the generations now present working together, honoring each other, and giving each other room to make mistakes, have successes, and be different from each other. Look at how the writer of Hebrews expounds upon this same theme, taking as his subject the fathers and examples of the faith that have gone before and linking them into the work of his own generation. *"And all these, having gained approval through their faith, did not receive what was promised, because God had provided something better for us, so that apart from us they should not be made perfect"* (Hebrews 11:39-40).

In the context of the "last days," nobody knows or can know the exact day or hour, and nobody really knows exactly how the history of mankind will end, though we all share many views about the sequence of events leading up to the end. We know that our Lord Jesus Christ will come again. This we know.

So, either this book and subsequent revelation of understanding is indeed for the very last of the last days, or in greater context, perhaps it is for just another generation in-between hundreds of others. Regardless, you are the "Joshua Generation." As we have seen already and will yet see, you are called to pioneer; to set the captives free and proclaim freedom to the ends of the earth.

The old and the young, working together like a family is to be for a true "end times" generation, so as we get closer and closer to the end of days, truly what Peter highlighted from the book of Joel and what Zechariah saw will be seen in greater and greater intensity.

What is the scriptural warrant for true end-times ministry? If you can catch the vision which this chapter is addressing, you will be able to better work towards the common good of all. Here's the vision: *God is building His family in the earth. He is building a special network of unique relationships.* These include, but are not limited to; fathers to sons, mothers to daughters, young men and women to other young men and women, uncles to nephews and aunts to nieces. The list goes on. I am speaking here of the spiritual connection between relationships and not so much a natural connection, though natural connections will and may exist.

X'ers long for true community. A community of committed relationships surrounding them where they can give and receive and be real with each other is what we are looking for. That is why small groups and cell structures work so well with our generation. In the smaller group setting, relationships can be built to a level of being able to be open, honest, and give and take. We can express our feelings and be challenged to change in a non-threatening environment. The less "man-made structure" the better.

And God is at the bottom of this deep yearning and answers it with the calling of young and old relationships together.

THE CRY OF OUR GENERATION

The cry of our generation is, "Love me. Just love me. Accept me for who I am." As an X'er reading this, even though all may look dark around you, rest in the fact that God does love you, through the love of His fatherhood and through the love of a

THE CRY OF OUR GENERATION IS, "LOVE ME."

risen savior. Find some others of like passion for Christ and reach out and begin relating to them. As a Moses, you must have the heart of compassion for the hurting, the downcast, the fatherless. Walk among those fields of the fatherless and dare to reach out. Dare to be a "father" or a "mother" in the faith to a "son" or "daughter," or if you can change your terminology a little, be an "uncle" or an "aunt" to a "nephew" or a "niece." The reason is that some in our generation shy away from the terms "father" or "mother" either because of our natural relationships having gone bad in those areas or because some well-meaning but controlling church leaders have tried to embrace us as a "son" or "daughter" only to end up stifling our growth. The terms "uncle" or "aunt" for the Moses generation will be better received, and we'll examine that more in the following section of this book.

In Stephen Spielberg's film, <u>Shindler's List</u>, the poster for the film shows the young, delicate, tender hand of a little girl with a red dress, being held comfortingly by a stronger hand of an adult. Without realizing it, Spielberg was prophetically giving us a photograph of end times ministry. The picture was a close-up of the two hands; of the older man holding the hand and protecting the young girl, with her tiny hand in his. The fate of the little girl is unfortunate and heart-breaking in the film, but the message rings loud like a clarion bell. The older generation holds the hands and helps the younger generation. Old and young, coming together.

We asked earlier in the book, "Am I my brother's keeper?" The answer: yes. This is also a picture of the grace of God. The word for grace carries a special meaning. The connotation is "bending over" and the stronger embracing the weaker. So in God's net of end-time relationships, the weaker strands must be held in place by the stronger ones. We all need each other and have to learn the hard way to work through relationship conflicts and personality issues to join hand in hand. One hand holding a staff like Gandalf, the other holding a sword like Aragorn.

What will come upon the latter church are the same external forces of persecution which came upon the early church, pushing her in seclusion and in the house-church settings. The large mega-churches, as we see them today, may not be standing twenty or thirty years from now, should Jesus tarry. The church will be forced by external pressures to exist underground. And the glory of the Lord will be upon her. And these kind of "house church" settings are where our generation will flourish.

Pressure Produces the Precious

What brought the real unity in the early church? It was pressure; pressure on them caused them to lay aside their differences and bond together. We will be like the armed forces coming ashore at D-Day in Normandy, France, in which each person, no matter what their color or age, will be needed to defeat the common enemy. It is high time we re-orient ourselves around our common Lord, and allow Him to commission us to fight our battles together.

In the film, Glory, which is based on historical truth, Colonel Robert Gould Shaw is portrayed as the young man chosen to train and lead the first black regiment in the American Civil War. At first, the black soldiers face persecution from the white soldiers. Also there is fighting and disputes within the ranks of the black unit, until their first day of battle. There, the black soldiers who had disagreements came together and saved each other's lives, and both black and white soldiers came together to defeat the common foe. External pressure brought a true heart-knit unity. Get ready.

Think about a pearl. What is a pearl? It is just a piece of sand that is pressurized over time in the stomach of an oyster to become (or, "producing") a valuable piece of jewelry.

Think about a diamond. What is a diamond? It is just a cheap lump of coal made valuable under pressure. In the last days God is going to have His pearls and His diamonds - a group of people made valuable by the pressures He allows and even forces at times upon His children. So, as one of my mentors, Larry Alberts, once put it in his seven "p's," "Pruning provides pain and pressure, producing precious people."

Some have prophesied sweeping changes for this world over the next few decades. There are prophetic words about war, financial instability, terrorism, the Spirit of Islam, and natural disasters. Great signs in the heavens and earth will cause men's hearts to fear. The Antichrist will arise, and as a one-world "religion" grows larger, increasingly tolerant, inclusive, and general, the

WHEN YOU JOINED THE RANKS OF GOD'S ARMY, YOU RELINQUISHED YOUR RIGHTS TO YOURSELF

remnant of true believers in Jesus Christ, followers of His Way, will grow more unified. Persecution will intensify. Then at the appointed time, Christ Himself will burst through the eastern sky, carrying with Him salvation for all who have endured and remained faithful until the end, and judgment for the souls of all the wicked who have forsaken Him. Until then, whether it is in our generation or in one that follows ours, we have a responsibility to be all that we can be for Jesus.

When you joined the ranks of God's army, you relinquished your rights to yourself, and surrendered your will to the will of God. You were a slave of unrighteousness, now you become a slave of His righteousness, a servant to His calling; you gave your very lifeblood, and it may be required of you in the end.

GOD'S HEART FOR THE HARVEST

God has a lot to say about the fields of the fatherless for the last days. The challenge of bringing lost sons and daughters to the bosom of the Father and thus harvesting the fields of the fatherless is set before us. And His word promises we will succeed. *"Return, O Israel, to the Lord your God, for you have stumbled because of your iniquity. Take words with you and return to the Lord. Say to Him, 'Take away all iniquity, and receive us graciously, that we may present the fruit of our lips. Assyria will not save us, we will not ride on horses; nor will we say again, 'Our god,' to the work of our hands; for in You the fatherless finds mercy.' I will heal their apostasy, I will love them freely, for My anger has turned away from them. Whoever is wise, let him understand these things; whoever is discerning, let him know them"* (Hosea 14:1-4, 9a).

One by one, X'ers are turning to the Lord. The gods of secularism and materialism are fallen, and the painful isolation that our generation feels is crumbling as we meet the truth of the love of the Father through relationship with the Son Jesus. Though you walk the earth on the fields of the fatherless, and masses of wayward sons and daughters fill the streets, it's time to begin to restore the streets and homes in which you live. That's right: to raise the banner of truth, and let it fly over the land. To boldly stand upon the word of God as your standard for righteousness and life. God's heart is to fill these fields with the old and the young, anointing both in unique ways to be bridge builders and relationship builders for the lost.

"I will pour water on him that is thirsty, and floods upon the dry ground" Isaiah 44:3. God is getting ready to poor his water on the dry grounds, and they shall become fruitful fields of harvest. The fields of the fatherless are becoming the fields of harvest.

However, they will only be fruitful fields of harvest if the Moses' out there will seek for God's new ways to bring up the next generation. Consider this sobering quote from Juan Carlos Ortiz. "Sometimes I think that no one of us is going to enter the new thing God is doing in this day. Because we come from Egypt, we are unused to the promised land, and may need to die in the wilderness; perhaps our sons must also. Then, free of tradition, our grandchildren can enter into the thing that God is doing in these last days."[34]

CHAPTER THREE

THE SPIRIT WHO POSSESSES YOU

"By the year 2010, 65% of the world's population will be eighteen years old or younger."[35]

"But My servant Caleb, because he has had a different spirit and has followed Me fully, I will bring into the land which he entered, and his descendants shall take possession of it" (Numbers 14:24).

The following chapter will continue in the focus of displaying the current generation we are in. This chapter goes further in casting vision and proving that the plans that the enemy had sown in evil, the Lord is turning around for good and that our greatest weaknesses are indeed becoming our greatest strengths. This chapter will focus on some "good news" as well!

THE WALKING DEAD

Nothing grieves the heart of this author more than the murder or assault of children. At Yad-Vashem, the Jewish Holocaust Memorial outside of Jerusalem, I once walked the cold corridors of the museum and viewed in horror the grisly photos of the atrocity. A separate memorial stands next to it in tribute to the two million children killed in the Holocaust. Their names are read over and over in continuous form, and their little photos are masqueraded on the projection walls, cascaded by thousands of points of star-lights which shine in the darkness.

At the entrance to the Memorial there is quoted a small passage of scripture from Lamentations. *"Better are those slain with the sword, than those slain with hunger; for these pine away, being stricken for lack of the fruits of the field." Lamentations 4:9.*

And in context of this passage, nothing in that Memorial moved me as much as a photo of a young boy, crouching in terror on a street corner. His hollow eyes were full of fear and glared into the camera lens. His tender hands clutched his little breast, exposed in the cold because of the lack of clothing. The rest of his rags clung about him, barely enough to cover his nakedness, let alone keep him the slightest bit warm in the cold of winter. He was starving to death.

I am reminded of another passage of scripture from the same book, *"My eyes fail because of tears, my spirit is greatly troubled; my heart is poured out on the earth, because of the destruction of the daughter of my people, when little ones and infants faint in the streets of the city. They say to their mothers, "Where is grain and wine? As they faint like a wounded man in the streets of the city, as their life is poured out on their mothers' bosom." Lamentations 2:11-12.*

There is nothing new under the sun. Children and young people today are suffering. Perhaps you, dear reader, are one who has been born in adversity. Perhaps you have known what it means to walk the streets, or feel hungry, alone, or unloved. There are millions out there like you.

DESTRUCTION OF THE INFANTS

In the year 1973 abortion was legalized. Now by various statistics, experts estimate that many millions of abortions have taken place in this nation and across the world since then. When I visited Israel a few years ago the statistic was sixty million.[36]

Never before has there been such mass annihilation of a generation than today. Satan is trying to destroy us in our infancy, before we're ever born.

Only two million Jewish children perished in the second world war, yet tens of millions more children of every background have died in abortions since then. Satan is crafty; he's our enemy, a murderer, and assailer of our souls. He's trying to destroy the Joshua Generation before they arise to do great

YOU'LL LOOK AROUND AND SEE A GENERATION WHO BELIEVE THEY ARE THEIR OWN GOD

exploits. *"...he was a murderer from the beginning, and does not stand in the truth, because there is no truth in him"* (John 8:44).

Multitudes, multitudes of those who are left alive are in the valley of decision. Look around and you'll see a generation who believe they are their own god. They've heard it all and seen it all from the time they were in grade school. The mass media, the internet, the information age has successfully drawn the young away from the truth. It is no wonder Jesus spoke of people who walk the earth without Him as "the walking dead." *"He who does not believe has been judged already"* (John 3:18).

Much of our media has become ungodly and unwholesome, sensational in its approach, to appeal to the lusts and ungodliness of the society which surrounds it.

The effects of this widespread rebellion of the society and the youth have crept into the church as well. Many churches have compromised in their message, becoming lukewarm and afraid of telling the whole truth as it is revealed in scripture.

A watered-down, man-centered gospel is preached in many evangelistic meetings and on television, which tickles the ears and soothes the conscience, lulling it into peaceful sleep, and making a tremendous lack of impact upon the culture in which we live. In Europe, many of the great cathedrals and buildings which once gave life to hungry believers now stand empty and destitute; many of them are rented out to secular organizations or turned into museums. Among us has grown up a generation - a generation who "knows not the Lord." An entire generation refocused on themselves. And the appeals from many pulpits sound like a sales call instead of a gospel presentation.

"The gospel of the kingdom is the Christ-centered gospel. But there is another gospel-the gospel we have been hearing these last centuries. It's the gospel centered in man and not in Christ, in the human and not in the divine. This gospel is a consequence of a humanistic tide that came on this world. The church let humanism come into her and now we have received this humanistic gospel-this gospel centered in man. I call it "the gospel of the offers," "the gospel of the big sales," "the gospel of the specials," where the preacher offers the people some incentive to accept Jesus. But we don't accept Jesus, it is He who accepts us. The preacher presents Jesus as the one who is knocking at the door, and he says to the people, "Please open the door to Him." So the man thinks that he is going to do Jesus a great favor if he opens the door for Him. That is the gospel of the offers. If you accept Jesus, the preacher says, you are going to have joy, peace, health, and prosperity. Such a gospel appeals to the interest of man, not the interest of Jesus."[37]

The amazing dichotomy in all this is that we have failed to give our generation the hard gospel. The kind of gospel that Jesus taught us was one in which we are called to give up all of our life in surrender to Him, and walk a hard, tight road in obedience to the great command of love which He ushered in. And here is where many mentors to Generation X have failed. This incredible spiritual vacuum devoid of truth and discipleship has been created. Now we need to fill it with strong messages of truth, and strong love and relationship to X'ers that crosses all the cultural boundaries and brings the reality of a life dedicated to Christ to the forefront.

GENERATION 'X' BECOMES GENERATION 'YES'

In the beginning of this first section of the book I mentioned the "good" news and the "bad" news. It is time for the "good" news! We are the world's future. If you can hear the cry of God's heart, He is saying, "These are the very ones whom I have selected for a unique destiny."

We are perhaps the generation that God in His eternal counsels has planned to arise and fulfill the final prophetic history before the return of His Son to judge the world in righteousness. We who are alive and under about forty years of age are a part of this generation of people. Of course, the possibility is that the uniqueness of this generation has nothing to do with the last generation of earthlings before the second coming of Christ, and that there are in fact possibly another one thousand generations to come after ours.

However, since the Lord has spoken some significant things about our generation, I'm going to go with the flow and set forth a book about us, in hopes that we are the final one. Just a hope, not a promise! *"Each age, it is found,"* writes Ralph Waldo Emerson, *"must write its own books; or rather, each generation for the next succeeding. The books of an older period will not fit this."*

In the early nineties the church I was based out of as an itinerant minister started a college/career group. There were a number of people who were too old to be a part of the youth group and didn't want to be a part of the singles ministry. One day three of us got to praying about a name for this group. We wanted something with some 'kick' to it; something that would assign itself as a part of our identification and would set us apart from the other ministries; also something that would encompass other individuals from other churches.

As we were together praying, suddenly the Lord dropped a name into my heart that appeared to fit, like a glove that slides onto the hand to keep you snug and warm in winter. As I spoke it out, it seemed almost too big. It was too broad to encompass just our small group of young people. Indeed, shortly thereafter the Lord began to speak to me about His plans for an entire generation of young people who are appearing on the earth in these days. He also spoke to me of the responsibility and accountability of those called and anointed to proclaim salvation to them as well as train and disciple them. The ones called to do this enormous task may be young or old; are you one?

> The world has come up with a term for us...
> *"Generation X"* - *"Generation Y"* - *"Millenials"*
> The Lord has come up with His term for us...
> *"The Joshua Generation"* - **"Generation YES"**

Yes! We are the Joshua Generation! The name itself is coined from the group of warriors that came forth under the leadership of Joshua to overthrow the Satanic wickedness of their day, lay claim to and possess the land, and receive the promises given only to the victors who battle to the end.

An intercessor in Charlotte, North Carolina recently shared with me of her prayers that God would turn this "Generation X" into "Generation yes" who would say YES! - yes to salvation, yes to eternal life, yes to the Captain of our salvation, yes to Jesus - and intimate, passionate devotion to Him.

For the terms in this book, as was mentioned in the introduction, we are defining this generation as anyone born in approximately the forty year period of 1960-2000. In the time of Joshua, it took 40 years to clear out the old generation and let their bodies die in the wilderness of wandering. God's judgment was one year for every day the spies were in the land, bringing back a bad report. Let's look for a just a moment at how the Joshua Generation came about so we understand its significance for today.

A DIFFERENT SPIRIT

"'As I live,' says the Lord, 'just as you have spoken in My hearing, so I will surely do to you; your corpses shall fall in this wilderness, even all your numbered men, according to your complete number from twenty years old and upward, who have grumbled against Me. Surely you shall not come into the land in which I swore to settle you, except Caleb the son of Jephunneh and Joshua the son of Nun. Your children, however, whom you said would become a prey—I will bring them in, and they shall know the land which you have rejected. But as for you, your corpses shall fall in this wilderness." Numbers 14:28-32.

This passage in Numbers tells us of incredible justice in the history of the children of Israel. Here were the people of God, assembled like an army, ready to go in and conquer and possess the land that God had promised them. They send in twelve spies to take a look at it, one man from each of their father's tribes, thus representing in godly order the whole of the people; and ten of the twelve bring back a bad report. Ten of the twelve looked to what they thought was an impossibility, for they failed to recognize that with God, all things are possible to him that believes.

As a result, the people rebel, and the hammer of God's justice falls. His decision is perhaps the single most incredible judgment in all the scriptures; every single adult from twenty years old and upward will die in the wilderness. Only the teenagers will live to eventually take the land and inherit the promises. Every adult will die; every adult, that is, except two: Joshua and Caleb.

> *"But Joshua the son of Nun and Caleb the son of Jephunneh remained alive out of those men who went to spy out the land"* (Numbers 14:38).

So two of the young men had a "different spirit" about them; these two looked not at the impossibility in the natural but instead looked only to God by faith believing that He could accomplish the things which He spoke.

This book is dedicated to all the young people in the earth who would believe the truth of the word of God for themselves and possess the "different spirit," and to all the leaders who would become mentors. Later we will examine the subject of both apprentices and mentors in the third section of this book.

An entire generation of older Christians are about to be left behind, and their corpses will fall in the wilderness; God's hammer is falling once again in this hour, and all those who refuse to hear His voice and obey will be forsaken, and left to eat the fruit of their own way.

But God is looking to the young - to those who are of the age that will accept His invitation to know Him intimately, and launch out in the Spirit and possess the inpossessable, believe

GOD IS WANTING TO TRANSFORM US INTO THE XTREME

the impossible, and live the radical life of faith on the edge of the frontier. He is wanting to transform us into the xtreme.

Our promised land is all that God has ordained for us to possess and walk in; it's choosing to advance the Kingdom in signs and wonders though older Christians may stand against it and speak against it; it's evangelizing the nations and discipling them; in short, it's fulfilling ALL the promises of Christ and the Apostolic command to expand the Kingdom of God. And this call is being placed on the shoulders of the young to enjoy a special commissioning for a season.

Next we'll examine a clue for God's prophetic purpose for our generation. It is a wonderful play on words. Just remember as you read it that there was something significant hidden under the "X" found on the treasure maps of the pirates in the old days.

X MARKS THE SPOT

The early followers of Jesus, who had experienced a true con-version and reformed their lives as a result, took upon them a secret symbol; it was imperative that they do so as their faith in Christ alone as Lord caused their very lives to be in danger as they no longer swore to Caesar as 'Lord' and thus their faith was illegal and punishable by death. So they developed a secret sign, if you will, to recognize each other and enjoy true fellow-ship in the midst of their crooked and perverse generation: it was the symbol of fish, and used the Greek letters, IXOUS.

In Greek, these letters spelled out precisely what they believed in. It is an *acrostic*, a term given and used quite frequently in the old days where each letter represents a word or picture. In this case, the letters were as follows: "I" represents Jesus, "X" repre-sents Christ, "O" represents God, "U" represents Son, and "S" represents Savior. Or, "Jesus Christ, God's Son - Savior!" So, the letter for Christ was the letter 'X'. The fullness of that word is, "ichthys," as in, "ichthyology" – the study of fish. Peter became a fisher of men, and this became a secret symbol, kind of like a mini-statement of faith. Another ancient symbol, used in the early church, was the letter X with a P through it (thank you prophet Bill Gates; modern-day Windows users would recognize "XP" as a popular symbol)! The X with the P intersecting was the Greek first two letters for Christ!

Without even realizing it, the world has come up with a name which prophetically speaks of the destiny and purpose for this generation...it is 'Generation X', the 'Generation For Jesus'! What glorious Divine irony!

Our generation is the treasure underneath God's map of destiny for the earth. X marks the spot! We are Generation Yes, and X marks the spotlight of yes to friendship; a friendship with the one who lived and died and lives forevermore. We are a generation of the friends of God.

JESUS MY FRIEND,
A FRIEND WHO STAYS CLOSER THAN A BROTHER

We are a generation who take the revelation of Jesus Christ as Friend more serious than our predecessors. He was sent to establish friendship with God, through the personal presence of the gift of the Holy Spirit. Yes!

The religious people of His day, the Pharisees, were into performance, but Jesus was into His Father's good pleasure; they were into rules, but Jesus was into relationship; they were interested in pleasing men, but Jesus was interested in pleasing His Father; they sought for slaves to proselytize, but Jesus sought for friends to provide for; they brought bondage, but Jesus brought breakthrough.

I remember the days when I was into performance. Like a good Pharisee, I desired to "do a good job" for the praise of men. For me, it was very deep, because as a child I experienced constant rejection from my peers. I was picked on daily, and sometimes even beat up. I reacted in a fleshly way, for I knew of no other way to react. I became the "class clown" and learned that by being funny and performing well, I could gain acceptance from others.

This continued throughout my Christian life, until I was in Bible Training School. It had never been dealt with, and roots went down real deep.

One night, I came back to my room and shut the door. I was sensing the presence of the Lord strong, so I got on my knees and began to pray. I opened up my Bible. My eyes landed upon a key verse in Luke 5.

"about this time the multitudes were coming unto Him, and desiring to be healed of their disease, but Jesus would often slip away into the wilderness to pray." Luke 5:15-16.

Suddenly, these words lit up like a Christmas tree within my spirit: and they stung with sharp pain of conviction. Jesus never sought ministry: He wasn't into performance. His heart's desire was only for fellowship with His Father, not "the work of the ministry."

I began to weep and cry out for mercy. The Lord brought me back through time, through all the incidences of my fleshly performance mentality; all of them seemed to flash in front of me in an instant of time, and I recoiled at them. They seemed so sinful, and so they were. God desires truth in the inward parts, and He did not create us as "human doings" but "human beings." We were made to fellowship with Him.

JESUS CAME TO RESTORE US TO THE HIGH CALL OF FELLOWSHIP AND FRIENDSHIP WITH HIM

Jesus came to restore us to this high call. It is the call of fellowship and friendship with Him. In a familiar passage of scripture, He says, *"Greater love has no one than this, that one lay down his life for his friends. You are My friends, if you do what I command you. No longer do I call you slaves, for the slave does not know what his master is doing; but I have called you friends." John 15:13-15a.* We can enjoy being in brotherhood with Jesus, and being friends of the bridegroom.

It was R.W. Emerson who once remarked, "The only way to have a friend is to be one." This reminds me of a youth meeting I ministered at in 1994. One of the young men had a word from the Lord. He said the Lord told Him that in this hour of the church, He wanted to be a friend, just a friend with all of His children. He went on to list the characteristics of a friend: a friend is one you love, one who knows your heartbeat, one who is honest, open. When a friend speaks and says a few words, you can finish the sentence. This is a true friend!

In Jesus' day, He was criticized for "hanging out" with the prostitutes and sinners. He was called, *"the friend of publicans and sinners" Matthew 11:19.* Why? Because He was just that; He was their friend.

At least two characters in the Old Testament, long before Jesus or the Holy Spirit was revealed, are called friends of God. Moses is said to have spent so much time in God's presence that his face began to glow. *"Thus the Lord used to speak to Moses face to face, just as a man speaks to his friend." Exodus 33:11.* Abraham perhaps is given the most honorable title a man or woman may attain in this life: not 'king' or 'president' or 'sir'...no, he's called by James, *"the friend of God" James 2:23.*

Let me ask a question. Can you think of any place in the Gospels where Jesus personally calls anyone His friend? We know He had friends; but does it say anywhere who is <u>called</u> His friend? Let's look at a common story from John and see a surprising truth.

"Now a certain man was sick, Lazarus of Bethany, the village of Mary and her sister Martha...the sisters therefore sent to Him, saying, "Lord, behold, he

whom You love is sick." Now Jesus loved Martha, and her sister, and Lazarus." John 11:1-3.

In the story, Lazarus is sick, and Jesus purposely waits a couple of days to go, for He knows that Lazarus must die in order for a powerful miracle to take place. The love that Jesus is talked about having is the love of a friend, a friendship kind of love. In Greek the term is *phileo*. This man was his friend!

"Our friend Lazarus has fallen asleep; but I go, that I may awaken him out of sleep." John 11:11.

Here is an astounding truth: the reason Jesus raised Lazarus was because he was his friend! It is the only place in the gospels where Jesus called anyone His friend! And therefore He had compassion and performed a miracle which revealed even more of the truth of God the Father; He is the resurrection and the life, because He will resurrect those who are called His friends to fellowship with Him for all eternity. We shall live in friendship with Jesus just like Lazarus did! We enjoy this kind of friendship now, through the companionship of the Holy Spirit.

Let me close this section with the true story from one of my mentors in the faith, Larry Alberts. He has a worldwide apostolic ministry, and at one point several years ago his father took ill with a stroke. The Lord offered him the privilege of taking personal care of his dad the remaining months of his life, so he stepped out of ministry to serve and honor his dad by taking care of him. One day, the nurse came over to help Mr. Alberts take a bath, and son Larry was out in the kitchen and heard the conversation. "I've been praying for you," his dad told the nurse. "For me? You mean you've been talking to God?" The nurse obviously was not a believer, and this dear Catholic man, a committed Christian barely able to use his powers of speech, replied, "Of course I talk to God. God is my friend. Don't you talk to your friends?" At this, the nurse didn't know what to say! It was so natural to this godly man. His prayer life was a conversation of speaking and listening to God. His best friend was Jesus. Only a couple of months after this incident Mr. Alberts went home to be with his Friend for eternity. The challenge for us in our generation is to develop our relationship with God, no matter what church background or denomination we have come from, into deep friendship. Jesus is our friend who sticks closer than a brother. And the friends of God will turn the fields of the fatherless into harvest fields of faith.

CHAPTER FOUR

MARCHING ORDERS

"The Signs of war...advance"—William Shakespeare,
Henry V, Act I, Scene 1.

*"Pass through the midst of the camp and command the people
saying...you shall cross before your brothers in battle array, all
your valiant warriors, and shall help them, UNTIL the Lord gives
your brothers rest, as He gives you, and they also possess the land
which the Lord your God is giving them..." Joshua 1:11-15.*

Okay. We've examined the root causes of how our generation has deteriorated into a cultural backwater. We've seen
that the fields of the fatherless are ripe for harvest. So what is
the next step? How about a practical chapter with biblical and
historical examples blended with a couple of modern stories to
stir you to action? Understanding the hopelessness of our times
in light of the hope of Christ is the key. It is *because* the culture
is so dark that the light will shine even brighter. Since you are
that light, let this chapter stir you up to make a personal com-

mitment and decision to take your rightful place of authority and advance Christ's kingdom in your own sphere of influence.

We'll look at what happened in the initial Joshua Generation and some special scriptural examples of young people God has used in unique ways. Then we'll look at how certain young men and women of certain generations have taken the call of God seriously and seriously kicked some butt for God. Finally we'll wrap up our whole first section of the book with, "X marks the spot: a spotlight on a generation." First then to Joshua, via the understanding given to Daniel, about spiritual war in continuous formation and fulfillment.

THE BACKDROP OF OUR AGE: WARRING UNTIL...

In a prophetic passage in Daniel we read,

"I kept looking, and that horn was making war with the saints and overpowering them until the Ancient of Days came, and judgment was passed in favor of the saints of the Highest One, and the time arrived when the saints took possession of the Kingdom..." Daniel 7:22.

What a most fitting prophetic passage for these last days. Now, wherever you stand on your end-time or kingdom understanding, let me say that I firmly believe this gives us the backdrop of the warfare we are engaged in: that there is an eternal struggle between life and death, light and darkness, morality and immorality, truth and falsehood, right and wrong, good and evil, and we are caught right in the middle of it.

We are called to be those who FIGHT and "take our possession." I believe God has ordained His young saints to be those who do just that in the coming days upon the earth. There is a world-wide, global war against the beast. It is the privilege of the saints to be used to destroy him and all his works and establish the Kingdom of God upon the earth.

Over in I Corinthians 15, we read,

"...then comes the end, when He delivers up the kingdom to the God and Father, when He has abolished all rule and all authority and power. For He must reign until He has put all His enemies under His feet. The last enemy that will be abolished is death." I Corinthians 15:24-26.

I wrote earlier about that last enemy. It is death. Yet there are a whole host of other enemies: enemies like the pride of man, the lust of the flesh, sickness and disease, demonic oppression, and the like. We are yoked together with Christ, and are called to pay the price and work towards a higher call of destruction. We are called to destroy all that is demonic, to put down all that is contrary to Christ and His cross, to put all of Christ's enemies

THIS IS HOW WE DESTROY THE ENEMY: WITH HIS LOVE!

under His feet, and thus usher in the realm of eternity. When Christ saw injustice and oppression, He countered it with justice and mercy. When He saw hatred, He countered it with love. When He saw the weak battered and cast down, He healed their wounds, (both physical and spiritual) and raised them up. This is how we destroy the enemy: with His love!

The picture of this in Corinthians is that of an army which is advancing. It is a reign of war, with Christ as our Ultimate

Warrior, and we as His battle array. We are coupled with Him, as a train is coupled car by car to its engine. We are connected to Him just as the train of His robe is attached around His neck and becomes a living, abiding part of Him.

In this passage notice the "when's." "When He delivers up the kingdom to the God and Father"; "when He has abolished all rule." If you think about that for a minute, when is the "when"? It is after, "until"! In other words, the reign of Christ in this era of the "last days" will continue until we, as His church and army, have done our job in freeing as many captives as possible from the hands of the enemy and destroying as much evil as possible with His goodness. So we are reigning with Christ and battling UNTIL all His enemies are made His footstool, *then comes the end*" (v.24a). We are like Neo freeing the captives of the Matrix.

Now let's put this in the context of our army of young warriors and their Joshua's and Caleb's to lead and inspire them.

"Pass through the midst of the camp and command the people saying...you shall cross before your brothers in battle array, all your valiant warriors, and shall help them, UNTIL the Lord gives your brothers rest, as He gives you, and they also possess the land which the Lord your God is giving them..." Joshua 1:11-15.

There you have it. A prophetic picture of the young warriors and the commission of the Moses-aged leaders to *"help them (the warriors) until..."*

Do you see it? We are preparing to battle the enemy, to be trained and helped by the elder leadership, in order to cross the river and possess the land, ultimately ushering in the return of Christ, which shall be our "rest." Is it possible that if each person responded to the call of God on their own life and launched out by faith in the supernatural every day that we, as a whole generation, could finish the job? That perhaps <u>we</u> could bring Christ <u>to us</u>?

> "Pass through, pass through, nor sit among
> The hosts encamped around.
> The glorious Victor paved the way,
> Put all His armor on you may.
> With shield of faith held well in view,
> Thy song ere long—'He brought me through!'"

> —Anonymous.

You are called to arise in this hour and take your stand: as a young person, to be trained and apprenticed to fight the enemy. As a Moses mentor, to train others to be strong and do great exploits. Let us examine further this point of the power of obedience in Christ's warfare. The power of launching out by faith in the supernatural. We'll look at examples from the scriptures, from previous generations and an example from the current generation.

THE RADICAL REVISITED

In this chapter I am writing to send a message of encouragement to all readers who would agree that the situation of spiritual lostness in our day seems fatal. As believers, how can we impact the culture? How can we live differently, act differently, and respond to the pressures of life when from all angles we are assailed to go the way of the world and thus the way to destruction? Here is one way: to look back at examples from other generations, at other periods of time when darkness swept over a culture and in spite of that the young rose up with the light they had been given and broke free themselves and broke others free. The scriptures are the first place to look.

"God calls and uses people of every age but in every generation of time and history His eye is especially upon young people," writes Moses mentor Phil Buekler in a newsletter, "when it was time to silence a blaspheming giant, God chose a teenager named David. When God wanted to deliver Israel from idolatry and the oppression of the Midianites, he called a young man named Gideon. When a nation in exile needed prophetic leadership, God raised up a no-compromise young man named Daniel. When the fullness of time had come for God to become flesh, for a Son to be given, God selected a godly teenage woman named Mary."

The next place to look is from history. I'd like to choose two separate historical examples of young people who made a difference and dared to stand up and be different in their calling: George Whitefield from the 1700's, and Rees Howells from the 1900's. Of course, you can look at dozens of young men and woman throughout history who made an impact before the age of thirty; people like Joan of Arc, George Fox (who founded the Quakers), Jonathan Edwards, and Hudson Taylor, just to name a few, who all were changing the paradigms of how to "do ministry" and impacting their cultures for Christ. I also have a personal story to add from a ministry trip in Ireland when I was three and twenty, and then we'll wrap up this section of the book.

HE LOVED THE WORLD THAT HATED HIM

If you study the revivals of the past five-hundred years, it will be difficult to find a greater example of a young man who advanced the Kingdom more than George Whitefield.

God moved on this young man and breathed the fire of revival into him, and set him aflame for His glory, bringing forth the gospel in power and sign and wonder, and allowing it to burn up any chaff in the way.

His name is all but forgotten now, yet he was the most popular preacher of his time, known in nearly every household in the blossoming colony of America, much as Rev. Billy Graham is known today. He once said, "Let the name of Whitefield perish,

GOD MOVED ON THIS YOUNG MAN AND BREATHED THE FIRE OF REVIVAL INTO HIM

that the name of Christ be magnified!"[38] Perish it has in our modern day, all but disappearing from history books.

He began his preaching after a solid conversion experience at the age of twenty, in 1734. In bed at 10 p.m. each evening and awake and in prayer at 4 a.m., his personal devotional life was quite a testimony of his character. A personal friend of John and Charles Wesley, his followers were the first to ever be called, "Methodists" and the name stuck. The Wesley's organized these early believers into "societies" which today we would call "house churches" or "cells" and the Methodist movement within the Anglican church was started. Whitefield pioneered the art of field-preaching, for the simple reason that the ministers of his day disliked him and his message and closed their pulpits from him. So he decided to preach everywhere! And the people came.

He traversed the American colonies on seven great sweeps of preaching and proclaimed the gospel over a thirty-year period, proclaiming Christ sometimes in sermons lasting three hours to whole towns and regions, two or three times a day, seven days a week. Thousands daily and weekly came and hung on his every word as he proclaimed the truth of Christ, His cross, and His judgment throne, and the necessity of a personal conversion experience. He was called by many the man who was most singly used to bring 'Christ' to the colonies, and awaken sleepy religiosity and spark it into living flames of devotion. One of his lifelong friends was Benjamin Franklin.

He was called the weeping evangelist, as in nearly every sermon he would put down his bible, throw his head back, and weep openly for the sins of the hearers in front of him, and their affront to the truth and holiness of God. The love of Christ poured out of him on their behalf. "You blame me for weeping," he said in 1750, "but how can I help it when you will not weep for yourselves, although your immortal souls are on the verge of destruction, and for ought I know, you are hearing your last sermon and may never have another opportunity to have Christ offered to you?"[39] The media of his day made fun of him and called him a fool; close friends abandoned him, and yet he kept on in his calling to preach. William Couper once wrote on Whitefield,

> "He loved the world that hated him: the tear
> that dropped upon his bible was sincere.
> Assail'd by scandal, and the tounges of strife,
> His only answer was – a blameless life.
> Paul's love of Christ, and steadiness unbrib'd,
> Were copied close in him, and well transcrib'd;
> He followed Paul – his zeal a kindred flame,
> His apostolic charity the same."

In 1739 he wrote, "Lord, teach me in all things simply to comply with your will, without presuming to say, even in my heart, 'Why do you?'" This prayer he lived. He went through trial and tribulation, even losing his only son, still an infant, in a carriage accident. That same day he continued preaching instead of attending the funeral, saying, "I remember once Matthew Henry, that old divine, said, 'weeping must not hinder sowing.'"[40] He continued preaching for a decade, converting thousands of people. He was said to have preached from a portable wooden pulpit to two million people during this time. Every time he got knocked down, he got back up and continued throwing punches in the fight of faith. He preached 18,000 sermons.

He died in the middle of a preaching tour on September 30, 1770, and is buried under a church in Newburyport, Massachusettes. In 1994, at the start of my own evangelistic ministry at age 24, I visited that site, hoping to see his grave-marker. The church was locked that day, so I sat down on the front steps, meditating on this man's life for Christ. At that moment, the Lord seemed to speak in my own heart, "Why seek ye the living among the dead?" It was as if the Lord was saying, "Yes, my servant Whitefield lived boldly and changed his generation for Me, but buried under this church are merely his bones. He is alive with Me now, and his life stands as a witness and a testimony for you to take up the challenge for own generation, before you too die and they bury your bones in the earth." Jesus said in Revelation 22:12 *"Behold, I am coming quickly, and My reward is with Me, to render to every man according to what he has done."* Each of you reading must answer the calling in some way as Whitefield did. You never know when the Lord will "come" for you.

When the weary wheels of life stood still at last for him in the autumn of 1770, his lifelong friend Charles Wesley (whom the author of this book is named after) wrote an epitaph which read,

> "He wills us in our partner's steps to tread,
> And, called and quickened by the speaking dead,
> We trace our shining pattern from afar,
> His old associates in the glorious war,

Resolved to use the utmost strength bestowed,
Like him to spend and be spent for God,
By holy violence, seize the crown so nigh,
Fight the good fight, our threefold foe defy,
And more than conquerors in the harness die."[41]

THE BENDING OF HITLER

In this chapter we are opening up truth that any person, who responds to the call of God in his generation, can do great exploits even in the midst of incredible warfare. Sometimes we are called to do these exploits when there is no natural war happening; at other times, we are called to exploits when all around us there is bloodshed and tribulation.

Let's turn for just a moment in the midst of understanding this and look at another real example from history of a young cadet who soon completed his training in Spiritual Boot Camp and

THAT WHICH WE ACCOMPLISH BY FAITH IN THE INVISIBLE REALM WILL COME TO PASS IN THE NATURAL ONE

launched out in one of the most dramatic faith walks ever recorded in the last generation.

The story comes from an extraordinary biography of a most unusual believer. He was just a simple young miner from Wales born in the late 1800's, called by God to follow The Way. He was unusual because he didn't get stuck in religious patterns of the flesh, but walked a walk led purely by the Holy Spirit. His name was Rees Howells. In his later years, after many adventures of walking in the Spirit, he became the leader of a Bible training school in south-west Wales in the United Kingdom. Norman Grubb, who chronicled the life of this great servant of God shared that as the threat of Hitler and the second world war approached in 1938, the Lord confronted Howells to raise up an army of young intercessors to battle in the heavenlies on behalf of the war in the natural. These intercessors would be the young cadets in the Bible school. So here we have both a Joshua and a Moses in one example. His first years were as a Joshua, and he learned the delicate and powerful art of intercession in his twenties and changed many lives in his thirties. Then later God called him to apprentice other young men and women in intercession. This is the backdrop of our story here.

In a meeting with his "troops" on March 19, 1938, Howells declared, ""Prayer has failed. We are on slippery ground. Only intercession will avail. God is calling for intercessors—men and women who will lay their lives on the altar to fight the devil, as really as they would have to fight the enemy on the western front." It was made clear that a soldier at the front has no say in where he goes and what he does; he cannot take holidays or attend to the claims of home and loved ones, as other people can. The Lord was telling them that if some would become bondslaves to the Holy Spirit, and would throw their lives into the gap (Ezekiel 22:30), He would give the victory and avert war. A large number of the staff and students made the surrender. "We came right through," said Mr. Howells, "and I knew from that time on Hitler was no more than a rod in the hands of the Holy Spirit."[42]

The students and staff got together for whole days of concentrated prayer, sometimes bursting into praise and worship sessions where the power of God would descend and assure them of the victory. "At the height of the battle," writes Grubb, "the one prayer that the Holy Ghost gave to the college through his servant was, "Lord, bend Hitler." A point came when that cry of travail changed into a shout of victory. The devil had to give way.

On September 30th of that year, 1938, the Munich Pact was signed. War had been averted for the time being. However, the question remained: What did happen to Hitler? The one person who was in a position to know was Sir Neville Henderson, the British Ambassador to Germany at that fateful time. In his book <u>Failure of a Mission</u> he makes the following significant statements describing the remarkable reaction in Hitler after signing the Munich Pact:

"Hitler felt irritated with himself. A section of his followers were always egging him on to fight England while (England) was militarily unprepared...His Voice told him that there could be no more propitious moment for a war than that October; and for once he had been obliged to disregard that Voice and to listen to counsels of prudence...For the first time he had failed to obey his Voice...He had acted on several occasions in direct defiance of the advice of his stoutest followers and of his army, yet the event had always proved him to be right. Until Munich. There, for the first time, he had been compelled to listen to contrary opinion, and his own faith in his Voice and his people's confidence in his judgment were for the first time shaken...'You are the only man," he said somewhat bitterly to Mr. Chamberlin, "to whom I have ever made a concession."[43]

The Lord had "bent" Hitler. Remarkable! Have you ever heard of that story in a news broadcast? Probably not.

GOD WAS GOING OVER

This may sound incredible, but you can read for yourself in Grubb's book how this one group of isolated Gen. X intercessors in the United Kingdom turned the tide of the war by their faithful intercession. They prayed through the campaigns in Dunkirk, the Battle over Britain, North Africa, Italy, and the D-Day landings. Whenever they felt the victory in the Spirit-realm, the victory came in the natural. Remember, behind all events in the natural there is a spiritual cause and solution.

This past summer was the 60th anniversary of D-Day, and I watched the live broadcast from France which commemorated the assault. In 1995 I had stopped in the north of France and visited the D-Day landing beaches at Normandy in-between ministry trips in France and England. I remember just pausing at certain points, and silently remembering of the great battles that had fought and won on that very soil in which I stood. I toured the museum at Bayeau, the first town to be liberated on June 6, 1944, and walked slowly and methodically through. The Lord apprehended me and asked me to look closely at the faces of the young men – men who were my age and younger when they landed here fifty years ago.

At one point I stopped and read a letter in one of the glass case-ments of a young man to his mother. He wrote, "Thank you for reminding me to pray. I am praying much. It really is helping...you know what I mean." Here was a simple letter to a mother back home - a godly, praying mother - and the simplicity of the exchange between the two melted me to the floor in tears.

Here were young men, my age and younger, who are now dead and gone. The reality of the eternal was drilled into me. The Bible declares that our lives are but a vapor, and then we are gone. Though we are young, we have a destiny.

Rees Howells reported the awesome sense of Divine intervention he felt on the night of D-Day during his intercession period. He read General Eisenhower's Order of the Day to the assault troops, "The hopes and prayers of liberty-loving people every-where march with...Let us beseech the blessing of Almighty God upon this great and noble undertaking." And beseech they did. He prayed, "...lay a burden on us; don't allow us to be slack. If Hitler had won, Christianity, civilization and freedom would have gone. O Lord, protect and keep our men! Don't allow us to pray any differently from what we would if we were on the front line. We do believe the end of this will be victory."[44]

The Daily Telegraph, a month later, reported that it was the only night the U-boats did not patrol the channel. The allies approached the beaches of Normandy with 4,000 ships and 11,000 planes, and never met a single plane or ship of the enemy! God had spoken to Mr. Howells, "**I am going over** (bold emphasis mine) and there won't be a setback."[45]

$40,000,000 DOLLARS OF DOPE

Now let us look at a more recent example from my own min-istry journals! I was a young missionary in my early twenties and headed to Ireland in 1993 for a six-week period of time to work with churches there in evangelism. During an outing for prayer one day, I felt compelled of the Holy Spirit to gather a group of prayer companions and travel to the Dingle Peninsula, in County Kerry, which is the western-most point of the whole of the nation of Ireland and the continent of Europe.

A group of eight of us assembled for prayer; we gathered in a circle and began to intercede for the nation. The very location of our small motley group seemed to be significant. On one side laid the wide-body of the Atlantic ocean, on the other, laid the land of the Emerald Isle and beyond it, England and Europe. Suddenly one of the members of our group got a vision from the Lord. He saw in the Spirit realm what appeared to be a very large ship coming near the shore. It looked dark, ominous, and very demonic. It was downloading some kind of evil cargo onto smaller boats, and these smaller boats were then taking it to shore and spreading its influence on the mainland.

We all suddenly felt a burden and began to intercede. We prayed a wall of fire around the nation of Ireland, and executed proper warfare and strategic prayer against the enemy, binding this influence from penetrating the border of water around the country.

Then we all went to our homes. I felt a sense of release, like our job had been done. It was now up to the angels of Heaven to fight on our behalf and do what needed to be done in the Spirit realm.

Three mornings later I was visiting Dublin and happened to look down at the daily newspaper, which read, "Twenty-Million

> **IT WAS RECORDED IN THE PAPER AS THE LARGEST SINGLE DRUG BUST IN THE HISTORY OF THE NATION**

Pound (that's about forty million U.S. dollars) drug bust off the shores of County Kerry."

Imagine! Here's what apparently had happened: a large ship, carrying two tons of cannabis resin (a heroine-type substance) had been downloading its cargo onto smaller boats just a day after our prayer time, which were then supposed to take the dope to shore, scatter it throughout Ireland, and then smuggle it to England and the mainland of Europe. But that night, a heavy fog rolled in, and the police were able to apprehend the culprits red-

handed before any of the cargo reached the shore! It was reported in the paper as the largest single drug bust in the history of the
nation, and it saved all of Europe from two tons of dope, most of
which would have been sold to young people. The Lord gave our
small group a part in thwarting the plans of the enemy.

The key here is that this group was just an ordinary small team
who decided to obey the leading of the Spirit, just as the group
from Rees Howell's Bible school did, and young George Whitefield
before him. And just like YOU can do if you only decide you're
going to launch out by faith and obey the call of God on your life.

X Marks the Spot: A Spotlight On A Generation

Christ is the center, or spotlight, of all we are about in this generation. The next section of chapters is more practical in nature.
As I mentioned toward the end of the introduction, it will be
helpful for our generation as it contains a series of exhortations
from the scriptures about living a radical lifestyle for Jesus in
spite of the culture around us. The themes of God as father and
the Church as our mother, character building, apprenticeship
and mentoring, and responding to the call, are included. This
section will also be helpful to those who are Moses' as it gives
examples of mentoring and what works and doesn't work in
affecting our generation for the gospel. It is written by a Gen.
X'er for Gen. X'ers and mentors, which is why it gives a special
focus to the trial and error ways of mentoring.

Gen. Xer's read ahead for practical advice as to how to get
where you desire to go in God! Mentors read ahead for tips to
apprenticing and releasing the next generation!

Consider these quotes as we close out section I of this book and
look to section II for further revelation. The first is an actual let-

ter from a young Joshua who gave his life for his country in the first World War. Consider the testimony of his faith, for he being dead, yet speaks. And consider if you have such a faith on the fields of this world. A faith that looks beyond the fatherless feeling of our generation and looks to the greatness of the One we serve and give our lives for. Our generation is looking for a cause worth dying for. The second quote stirs our hearts as one line of a famous hymn which the preceding generation sang. It's time for our generation to lift our battle songs.

Last letter from a soldier on the firing line in 1915.

"I feel the Master's presence very strongly, and I know He is with me, to guide, keep, and strengthen me, and I also know that if I have to go, I go to be with Him in glory, and this comforts me. What a grand thing it is to know you are saved, and your sins (though red as crimson) are as 'white as snow.' If I should not return, and it is quite possible that I will not, will you please keep my large Bible in remembrance of one who always tried and failed until he grasped the fact of remission of sins through our blessed Lord. Yours, Gunner W. Owen, RFA."

So whoever you are, and whatever category of warrior God has called you in, read on to formulate a plan to be trained in Boot Camp and released in your own special missions!

"Lead on, O King Eternal,
The day of march has come—
Henceforth in fields of conquest,
Your tents shall be our home:
Thro' days of preparation,
Your grace has made us strong,
And now, O King Eternal, we lift our battle song."[46]

ABBA & MAMA

"As for me and my house,
we will serve the Lord."

— *Joshua 24:15b*

CHAPTER FIVE

WHO'S YOUR DADDY?

"The climax of the whole Bible is the revelation that God is Father." –J.I. Packer

> "...you saw how the Lord your God carried you, just as a man (father) carries his son..." Deuteronomy 1:31.

In the two chapters of this section, the aim is to get you thinking as to the revelation of God's character and attributes as containing the fullness of "fatherly" and "motherly" qualities, being readily available to you through the "church", by the power of the Spirit. And to what end? The truth is, too many in the younger generation have never learned experientially to live with God as father and mother, because many have never had either the authority and discipline and love of a godly father or the compassion and nurture and love of a godly mother.

Throughout scripture God has ordained the influence of the next generation to be both patriarchal and matriarchal, both in natural and spiritual influences. If one or the other are over-emphasized or de-emphasized, there is imbalance. And of course our western culture hasn't helped with all the current negative stereotypes in the media of what fathers and mothers look like. Our culture is a hodgepodge and a mess with ungodly beliefs about natural and spiritual parenting.

Also, many in the older generation want to take the place of the Lord in their mentoring, instead of understanding the revelation from the scriptures that there only is one Father (who encompasses both the attributes of father and mother all in one person), who is meant to be the One we point the way to in our ministries and our raising up of the next generation. These chapters guide all – mentors and apprentices – to the One True God and His revelation in both testaments as having the attributes of "father and mother," and the application of the "church" becoming our "mother" through the Spirit. So the first chapter will discuss God relating to you as your "father" and the second will encompass the church relating to you as your "mother." Let's begin this theological journey as looking through scripture and finding God revealed in both "fatherly characteristics" and "motherly characteristics."

EARTHLY MEETS HEAVENLY

I guess I was one of the lucky ones. I grew up in a home where my dad and mom loved me and showed their love for me. They disciplined me from time to time, but it was always in love.

I realize my case was the exception, not the rule. Many in this generation have grown up or are growing up without the blessing of a father who loves them and disciplines them in love or a mother who nurtures and cares for them in the home. Perhaps you are one of these people.

On a recent ministry trip through Germany, I sat with a Christian man and listened as he related his story. He was in his mid-thirties now, but had spent most of his life addicted to drugs and alcohol. He had been in and out of several gangs and nearly killed at least a half-a-dozen times. Although he had committed his life to the Lord when he was a teenager, he had spent most of his days in addiction (because of his bruised childhood).

He related to me what it was like to grow up in a home where his father abused him and his brother, and later left them with no explanation. His mother didn't spend much time with the children after that. "I hate him. I've forgiven him, but I still hate him. The son of——." Tears welled up in his eyes as well. We sat and prayed together. He was on his way to a hospital, where he was making a fresh commitment to get off the drugs and be rehabilitated.

Sadly, the images of his earthly father and mother had marred the image of his Heavenly one. And this may be the case for you, dear reader, whoever you are.

NO MATTER WHAT YOUR AGE, ONE OF THE AREAS OF HEALING IN YOUR LIFE MUST BE IN THE WAY YOU VIEW GOD

As we already looked at in the first section of this book, part of the earthly father's role is to mirror the love, nurture, and discipline of the heavenly Father, and the mother is meant to raise the children with compassion, care and also discipline, but if they failed or fell short in any of these areas, (as all parents do in one way or another), then your image of God the Father will be marred. It will reflect the image and characteristics of your earthly parents. There is no getting past this.

No matter what your age, one of the areas of healing in your life must be in the way you view God, and thus, in the way and manner in which you choose to relate to Him. Do you see Him as an old, white-bearded tyrant, who sits in Heaven and judges every little mistake you make? If so, you have a misconception of Him. He created both Adam and Eve, and they were made in His image, which means that within the sphere of His character exist all the positive traits of both fathers and mothers, men and women.

This truth cannot come merely from intellectual knowledge. No, it must come from the Lord, who, by the revelation of the Holy Spirit, brings to light these truths and melts them into your heart, as you experience His love – the love of your Lord. Whether you are young or old, a Joshua/Caleb or a Moses, you need to affirm God as Father to us all with His "motherly compassion."

So the logical place to begin is to look at the truth of God as He reveals Himself in both the Old and New Testaments: as God who is both a father and mother in His attributes. Let's begin with the "fatherly" attributes.

GOD MY FATHER, A FATHER EVER PRESENT

Throughout the whole of the Old Testament, God revealed Himself to His people as a Father. They were called "the children of Israel" because they were just that - children who had a common parent, God Himself.

One thing to keep in mind is that although the writers of both

Testaments are of course human, God is revealed as essentially Spirit in nature, and to better understand Him, writers of scripture used terms and pictures like physical body parts (i.e. the right hand of God, the mouth of the Lord, His ears are open to your cry, etc.). But these are just finite terms and there is an element of mystery in all of this. So the following development of God with parental qualities is not an exhaustive study. It is merely an analogy to picture God in a certain light for our generation which has been raised without many godly parents and thus an understanding of His parenting qualities is lacking for many. Remember as you read these scriptures that there is still a great mystery and reverence in the realm of faith to relate to God. We must continue to live in the universal paradox of God as incomprehensible and utterly majestic and God as very comprehensible and utterly personal.

It was forbidden to speak the name of the Most High. Instead, He revealed His character and His attributes through the various names He was called by. Each name revealed a new portion of understanding of His character as the God who provides, leads, and protects. For example, when Abraham was about to sacrifice his son of promise in Genesis chapter 22, suddenly there appears a ram caught in the thicket, and Abraham is able to sacrifice the ram instead of his son. So he names the place The Lord Will Provide, or Yahweh (Jehovah) Jireh. This shows us the portion of God's character as a father who provides for His children in their time of need. Later He revealed Himself as The Lord Your Healer, or Yahweh (Jehovah) Rophe, as Moses turned the bitter waters of Meribah into sweet waters and God healed the diseases of the people as they began their journey toward the promised land in Exodus chapter 15. Then a couple of chapters later, Joshua and a group of soldiers fought against Amalek, and as Aaron and Hur held up the hands of Moses, they won the day. Then Moses built an altar, and named it The Lord is My Banner, or Yahweh (Jehovah) Nissi. This revealed another part of God's character - His justice in destroying the wicked and bringing strength to the righteous. He is our provider, our healer, our banner, and the list goes on. As a loving Father, He doesn't want to see His children in lack, or sick, or without victory against their weakness. No father would!

God has always distinguished Himself from all the other gods through being personal. One of His names as revealed in the Old Testament is, "Yahweh." This is a personal name for God, which

"THE ONE WHO GOD IS, IS PERSONALLY, PERPETUALLY PRESENT."

translated means, "the one who is" or you could say, "the I am," or, "The One Who is Always Present." He is a personal God with personal relationship to His creation, and in the present tense. He always "was, is, and will be" and that revelation is in the context of now. In Deuteronomy He gives a beautiful picture of Himself as a Father through Moses. It says, "...you saw how the Lord your God carried you, just as a man (father) carries his son..." Deuteronomy 1:31.

This understanding completely changes the relationship that human beings have in their creator. Every other religion on the face of the earth at the time of Jesus had a multitude of gods, but none of them revealed themselves as being, "personal." God's revelation to His people Israel was unique, and then His revelation through His son, Jesus Christ, was even more unique, and it's been unique ever since. It's one of the main themes that sets us as believers in Jesus apart from every other belief or creed or worldview.

God considered and called both the nation of Israel and Jesus His 'son'. In Exodus chapter 4, He says to Moses, *"Then you shall say to Pharaoh, 'Thus says the Lord, "Israel is My son, My first-born. So I said to you, 'Let My son go, that he may serve Me,' but you have refused to let him go."*

Much later in history, long after Israel obeyed God and then had forsaken obedience to God for the practice of idolatry, He speaks through the prophet Hosea. He says in chapter 11, *"When Israel was a youth I loved him, and out of Egypt I called My son."* If you read the whole of the chapter you'll find some interesting phrases. *"Yet it is I who taught Ephraim how to walk, I took them in my arms," "I led them with cords of a man, with bonds of love," "I bent down and fed them."* Can you hear the heartbeat of God the loving Parent, who is revealing himself as a sad father who watched his only son disobey and turn to rebellious ways? *"So my people are bent on turning from Me." Hosea 11:7.*

In this chapter of Hosea, God speaks tenderly of his deep love for Israel, comparing it to the love a father for his disobedient child. He had remained faithful to them though they were faithless. Now, despite his great reluctance to do so, He must punish them with exile into Assyria instead of Egypt. *"They will not return to the land of Egypt; but Assyria — he will be their king, because they refused to return to Me." Hosea 11:5.*

The gospel writer Matthew applied Hosea 11:1 to Christ. *"And he arose and took the Child and His mother by night, and departed for Egypt; and was there until the death of Herod, that what was spoken by the Lord through the prophet might be fulfilled, saying, "Out of Egypt did I call My Son." Matthew 2:14-15.* So God called both Israel and Jesus His son, and ironically both lived for a time in Egypt. Matthew's use of the passage shows the beautiful identification of the Son of God with the historical people of God. Both had a unique relationship with the Father of lights, in whom there is no variation or shadow of turning. God even spoke audibly to Jesus at His baptism and said those wonderful words, *"This is My Son, in whom I am well-pleased."* Remember this truth from that incident: the encouragement from Dad and acknowledgement of the identity of Jesus came before Jesus actually did any miracles or ministry!

His identity was first to God His Father, unrelated to His ministry for His Father's glory. You are first a son or a daughter of the Most High irregardless of whether you ever do any kind of ministry for Him!

He created all mankind, and yearns to be near them and reveal Himself to them, but the only way now for a person to receive

THE ONLY WAY NOW FOR A PERSON TO RECEIVE THE REVELATION OF HIS FATHERING AND MOTHERING HEART IS ACROSS THE BRIDGE OF THE LORD JESUS CHRIST

the revelation of His fathering and mothering heart is across the bridge of the Lord Jesus Christ.

THE TWO ESSENTIAL INGREDIENTS

One of my favorite foods is one that I owe to my childhood: the peanut-butter-and-jelly-sandwich. Now apart from the bread, there are two essential ingredients: peanut butter and jelly. Without jelly, it's just peanut-butter, and would stick to the top of my mouth. Without peanut butter, it wouldn't have the same flavor. The jelly would be too sweet. Both are definitely needed on the bread. It takes the loving blend of a mother and a father to make a baby and raise him or her in the fear of the Lord. In the same way, it takes two ingredients within Yahweh, as both father and mother towards mankind, to bring balance and proper growth to the children.

There are two essential ingredients, or attributes, which make Yahweh so good and are revealed in the previous passage from Hosea - love and discipline - both mixed together around the bread of His authority.

These two attributes are essential. He loves us, and because He loves us, He disciplines us. There are two kinds of love that God flows in as God the Father – soft love and hard (or, tough) love. The hard love is like the discipline of a strict but godly father protecting His kids, who disciplines them in tough love for their own good. The soft love is the gentle, abiding, compassionate love which He pours out; it is like the love of a mother for her children. Both are absolutely central to God and must be present in order for there to be balance. When both are not there in the formation of any young life, natural or spiritual, imbalance and problems will follow.

My first roommate in college was an example of soft love without hard love in natural childhood development. He and I were eighteen years old when God put us together as roommates at a Lutheran liberal arts college in Western Minnesota. I'll never forget him. He was the most spoiled, rebellious, "silver spoon" I had ever met. He was very good at brown-nosing any adult, yet his personal life was a mess. He had no discipline; he always wanted what he could not have, and became a cry-baby when he didn't get it. He was eighteen in body but eight in maturity. He had been shaped by a lifestyle of growing up with no discipline. As I recall he was very close to his mother and very distant from his father.

For an example of natural hard love without soft, think of the hard Colonel von Trapp in, "The Sound of Music." Do you remember the von Trapp children? Their father was a strict disciplinarian. He would blow the whistle, and then all the kids would line up for inspection. Then it was a blowing of the same whistle for them to go off to bed, and on went the cycle. There was no real relationship with his children. He loved them, and chose to raise them in this strict manner, but was emotionally unattached and consequently the whole family was unbalanced. Young Maria comes into his life to bring that soft edge. This is the balance that any Father must have, the ability to be a Father who disciplines, and a Friend who loves.

I had both, though it was hard.

I remember once I disobeyed my parents quite deliberately when they were away for a week at their annual spring convention. I did something really bad to my sister. I don't even remember what it was, but it must have been pretty bad, because, when my parents arrived home, my sister went "crying to mama." Boy was I in for it!

I'll never forget. My dad was so upset; he got the family Bible, turned to Exodus 20 and the Ten Commandments, shut me up in my room and gave me strict orders to write the fifth commandment fifty times, in perfect straight rows with perfect penmanship. If I got one word wrong, he would tear it up and I would have to start all over again. Boy, was I nervous and scared. Proper discipline will almost always be painful for the time.

So I sat and I wrote. And wrote. And wrote. I still can recall to this day the King James Version of the commandment, *"Honor thy father and thy mother, that thy days may be long in the land which the Lord thy God giveth thee.*" Believe me, this event made an impact.

It took me three whole hours to do it. Still trembling, I slowly slipped down the steps and into the family room and showed it to my dad. "Looks good. You're forgiven," he said, then gave me a hug and kiss.

Believe it or not, this is the way of God the Father as well. Let's turn to a passage of Scripture which addresses this.

"You have not yet resisted to the point of shedding blood in your striving against sin; and you have forgotten the exhortation which is addressed to you as sons, "My son, do not regard lightly the discipline of the Lord, nor faint when you are reproved by Him; for those whom the Lord loves He disciplines, and he scourges every son whom He receives." It is for discipline that you endure; God deals with you as with sons; for what son is there whom his father does not discipline? But if you are without discipline, of which all have become partakers, then you are illegitimate children and not sons. Furthermore, we had earthly fathers to discipline us, and we respected them; shall we not much rather be subject to the Father of spirits, and live? For they disciplined us for a short time as seemed best to them, but He disciplines us for our good, that we may share His holiness. All discipline for the moment seems not to be joyful, but sorrowful; yet to those who have been trained by it, afterwards it yields the peaceful fruit of righteousness." Hebrews 12: 4-11.

Here is a powerful New Testament passage which ties together his same attributes as a Father to His children for both covenants and for His children for all time. Just as this passage mentions, I respected my dad even more after he disciplined me, for I knew that it was in love that he acted the way he did and wanted to see me grow up as a man of obedience, character, and strength. So God as my father saw to it that in my natural development at home, I was disciplined. He is just as ready to show this kind of tough love through His leadership in His

Church, when it is tempered with mercy, so that His spiritual sons and daughters learn His ways.

EVE WAS ADAM'S HELP, AND GOD IS OURS

For another example of God revealing His essential character in both soft and hard love we can go all the way back to the beginning in the garden of Eden.

Back in the garden, God had established His creation. Everything was initially made to perfection; everything had an order and a purpose. God created Adam and Eve that He might have someone to love. Human beings, made in God's image, are the greatest object of His love in all creation. We are the crowning glory of all that exists, both in the spiritual and the natural realms.

He had established His rule in the heart of both Adam and Eve, and His intent was to have all of His created order be in perfect unity with Himself. He had set the stage to be ruling in the midst of His people - in their hearts - throughout history.

You can read the whole account for yourself, Genesis 1-3. In essence, man initially had perfect fellowship and communion with God in the Spirit, but then through the deceitfulness of the snake in causing Eve and then Adam to sin, he chose to go his own way, causing death - the separation from God in which we find all human beings suffering from even to this day.

One of the central points in the story as relating to our theme of God as father and mother, is found in chapter 3, verse 8. *"And they heard the sound of the Lord God walking in the garden in the cool of the day."*

What is remarkable about this passage is the context. It is immediately after the fall of man. Adam and Eve had just disobeyed God and listened to the voice of the snake in the grass. They had willfully eaten of the Tree of the Knowledge of Good and Evil instead of the Tree of Life, and out of shame hid themselves from God's presence. His creation had fallen. He knew they had sinned and disobeyed Him, yet here we see the picture of the Parent seeking fellowship with His fallen son and daughter. The original Hebrew word for 'cool' of the day is

YET HERE WE SEE THE PICTURE OF THE PARENT SEEKING FELLOWSHIP WITH HIS FALLEN SON AND DAUGHTER

'wind' or 'spirit'. He was just coming to them in the way that He was accustomed to: in the spirit of the day. To God the Parent, it was just another encounter of fellowship with His children. And even though he had to have known what had just taken place, He still comes to them, reaching out in love.

It is a picture of the soft love. Then in the spirit of discipline, he shows His hard love. He immediately sets the situation in order and pronounces punishment and metes out proper justice for the offense, turning first to the serpent and then to Adam and Eve. Again, still later in the story, we see the hints of His fatherhood toward his now rebellious son and daughter in making them animal skins to clothe themselves. Most scholars point to this as the first sacrifice of animals and the shedding of blood as a type of the forgiveness of sins in scripture. His desire is still to be in relationship with us, even though, *"all have sinned and fallen short of the glory of God." Romans 3:23.*

Back to Genesis 3, Verse 9 is the clincher: *"Then the Lord God called to the man, and said to him, "Where are you?"* And this is still the call of His heart in the twentieth century and beyond into the twenty-first. He is calling out to His creation. He is calling to you and me for fellowship and companionship. The Lord is calling for His lost sons and lost daughters. His disciplinary right as Father of all Creation under girds everything He does...and his love is displayed in soft and hard ways daily. The kindness of God the Father leads us to repentance.

In the creation of Adam we have the creation of an earthly father. In the creation of Eve we have the earthly mother. Both form an expression of oneness that God desired to model His eternal attributes as both Creator and Sustainer of life. Eve is named prophetically by Adam in Genesis 3:30. Her name means, "life giver" or "life." She is the mother of all living. Martin Luther comments, "When Eve was brought unto Adam, he became filled with the Holy Spirit, and gave her the most sanctified, the most glorious of appellations. He called her Eve, that is to say, the Mother of All. He did not style her wife, but simply mother, mother of all living creatures. In this consists the glory and the most precious ornament of woman."[47] "Of particular note is the fact that Eve is created as a "suitable helper" (Heb., *'ezer*) for Adam (Genesis 2:18-22). The word does not imply subordination or inferiority, but identity, for only a being with the same personal capacities and capabilities as Adam could have related to him (God Himself is called a "help" (*'ezer*) in Psalm 46:1 and elsewhere).[48] Here is more evidence of God allowing Himself to be distinguished with both male and female qualities, both fathering and mothering qualities. Since mankind flowed out of the image of God, and mankind consists of both male and female, we can deduce that all of God's full character encompasses the best of both sexes. The same word of "helper" in the original language is used for Eve as well as for Yahweh! Of interesting note is another passage from Isaiah.

"For thus says the Lord, "Behold, I extend peace to he like a river, and the glory of the nations like an overflowing stream; and you shall be nursed, you shall be carried on the hip and fondled on the knees. As one whom his mother comforts, so I will comfort you; and you shall be comforted in Jerusalem." Isaiah 66:12-13.

To sum up, God is revealed in the fullness of attributes with both fathering qualities and mothering qualities. Now let's get radical for a moment: let's assume for now that His church, the remaining tabernacle of His actual presence on earth, is indeed meant to be our expression of mother.

CHAPTER SIX

BIG MAMA'S HOUSE

"But we proved to be gentle among you, as a nursing mother tenderly cares for her own children." I Thessalonians 2:7.

"Oh Jerusalem, Jerusalem, the city that kills the prophets and stones those sent to her! How often I wanted to gather your children together, as a hen gathers her brood under wings, and you would not have it!" "And when He approached, He saw the city and wept over it." Luke 13:34, 19:31.

I know that this chapter title has caught a few readers a little off guard. The case will now be proven for the "church" on earth revealing herself, through the Spirit, as our mother. All the earth belongs to God. In a sense, because of the creation, by Jesus, of His Church, we're all living in big mama's house.

His first words in creating His house on earth, the house of compassion and love to each other, cultivated in Divine intimacy, and with an outflow of love and compassion to the world, were incredible words. Words which had never been uttered by an individual in the history of mankind, and never could be uttered by anyone but a true god-man; the words were, *"All power is given unto Me in heaven and earth. Go therefore, and make disciples of all nations..." Matthew 28:18-19a.* These are words of power! Christ commands His special family to become the unique force in the earth of change. The compassion He felt over Jerusalem (in true motherly spiritual force) He still feels for the world which He created. And the "church," His special "called-out ones," are

VERY LITTLE HAS EVER BEEN WRITTEN OR TAUGHT IN THE CHURCH ABOUT THE CHURCH AS "MOTHER"

meant to demonstrate the Motherhood of the created order to you, the disciple.

Very little has ever been written or taught in the church about the church as "mother." In fact, in the void of scriptural understanding of this theme, the world has taken the idea to the extreme and feminist groups have taken up the cause in writing several popular books in our culture about God being a woman! Even some of the ancient religions in the older cultures believed pagan half-truths about God and made Him a Her and even created the term, "mother earth" to coincide with their limited understandings. This chapter starts something of a dialogue for you as a reader to consider and start to love the Lord with all your heart and receive His love, the love of God as Father, through His people on earth, His love with motherly attributes, through your older brothers and sisters around you comprising the church.

CHRIST'S CHURCH OUR MOTHER, A MOTHER EVER NURTURING

In the previous chapter, we saw the One God, who is revealed in Three Persons: Father, Son, and Holy Spirit, as containing, within all three of those Persons, both "fatherly" and "motherly" attributes. This chapter brings forth the understanding that you, as a reader, have an awesome, almost untapped capability as application to these truths: the capability of giving and receiving "motherly" qualities, through the Spirit, to and from the other members of Christ's church around you. The true "community" and "relationship" that our generation needs and longs for is only found in the church. She herself is God's expression of compassion to her members and to the world on this earth. She is the focus of God's highest attention and her growth is His highest priority, both now and to the ending of this age.

Thus, though you may have lacked a good foundation of relationship with your own earthly dad or mom, theologically speaking, the Lord Himself embraces you in all your manhood or womanhood and grants you the full identity of being a son or daughter to Himself, and then in the relationships around you He pours out a motherly embrace for you to walk in health as a warrior and give healthy relationships to others who need the compassion and love you have received.

For an interesting side-note, consider the inner-city gangs of our day, with their graffiti messages tattooed on the buildings and train stations around us, as the satanic counterfeit to the church as God's mother in the Spirit. The gangs of our day emulate a kind of false love and acceptance, which cult-like, end in control and manipulation. Opposing this, in many sectors of our society, a true expression of Christ's church is being displayed, with members living out the historical realities of the early chapters in Acts when she was first-born. Your mother, through the Spirit, is meant to be the compassion and love flowing through your brothers and sisters all around you. The hurt, the insecure, the lonely all join gangs looking for a filling of the void inside. Instead, if the church on earth would arise to become Big Mama's House, the atmosphere of family would be generated to such an extent as to cause great transformation.

Here are some attributes of a human, godly mother which Christ's church, through the instant access of the Spirit within the older believers around you and within yourself, contain and release to each other (with the analogy of a mother to her newborn):

ACCEPTANCE. Every godly mother on earth has an instant acceptance of their baby. The ties that bind are strong and cannot be easily broken. The church is called to walk in acceptance of each of it's members, no matter what the theological differences may be that try to separate. The ground is level at the foot of the cross, and acceptance for who we are is the starting point in our relationship to God as Father and His Church as Mother. Your other brothers and sisters accept you for who you are, and because of what Christ has made you. Baptism, one of the two rites which Christ gave the church, is the outward form of the inward reality of our true acceptance with God, through our identification with Christ and His blood, and with each other, the community of saints around us to support, love, and nurture us on earth. A mother sees and knows your faults, but loves you and lives with you in spite of them, through her acceptance.

VALUE. Every godly mother values intensely their own baby. Again, this is based on relationship. That baby is bone of her bone, and flesh of her flesh. The mother values intensely the gift of life of her child for who the child is, not for anything the child has done. The church, through the Spirit, mirrors value as mother to child because we all have become bone of Christ's bone, and flesh of Christ's flesh, through the Spirit, and brought forth in relationship, every time we partake of the communion table. Communion, or sharing of the bread and wine as Christ instituted to the church, identifies us with value as sons and daughters. We were valuable enough in Christ's heart for Him to sacrifice His very life, and we receive His nature and transmit value to each other through becoming One with Him.

<u>CORRECTION AND DISCIPLINE</u>. Every godly mother knows and understands the value of discipline in raising her child. Whatever cultural form or expression it may take, correction brings a fruit of righteousness to a child. Even so, the church is called and committed to correcting herself, through the Spirit. Other sections of this book cover this theme more closely. As you begin to relate to Christ's church as your mother, be open to the correction of your brothers and sisters in love, and walk in a continual posture of change, which in the long run, causes you to bear more fruit for Christ.

<u>HEALING</u>. A godly mother kisses the "owie" of the child and brings instant healing! Guess what? Christ's church, as your mother through the Spirit, can heal herself (so to speak, through the blood and power of the name of Christ at work)! The church is called to a most unique function in the earth: a healing hospital, where its own members can receive physical healing through the believing prayers of each other, and those who are hurt in the world can receive healing through the compassionate hands of the church as our mother. The world really is Big Mama's House, a place where, since the Kingdom has come (though not yet in her fullness since her King has not yet returned) she can walk about like a mother with the kiss of heal-

ing for every "owie" that exists, either for her own members or the world's unbelievers. We have more authority on earth than we realize. Begin to believe that the church around you has the motherly capability of healing prayer, through faith in Christ, to touch every area of need in your body.

ROOTS AND WINGS. Once my spiritual mentor Dorothy Langstaff said to me, "There are two things you can give your children in this life: roots and wings." Every godly mother knows this by instinct. She gives instruction and training to her child, then at some point releases that child to soar in the skies. The church, through Christ, is our mother, to give us roots of historical theology, scriptural understanding, and training in Christ's righteousness. Whether you attend a home fellowship, a mega-church, a bible school, a seminary, or some other expression out there, you are filled with Big Mama's instruction about Christ and the Kingdom through the Spirit. Yet at some point, the mentors around you need to have the spiritual insight and foresight to release you from the nest and let you test your wings to fly. Other sections of this book talk more about this in fullness, so read on to be released through your mother and become a mother to those around you! The discipled become the disciplers.

ABOUT FATHER'S BUSINESS

Think for a moment about Jesus' life. His first priority was relating to God as His Father; this He learned to walk in very early. He was raised in the ideal way for any of us to be raised; first, under the authority of his spiritual father, and second, under the authority of his natural parents. This caused the proper formation of character for Him. He submitted to his natural father and mother along with His Heavenly one.

"And He said to them, Why is it that you were looking for Me? Did you not know that I had to be in My Father's business? And He went down with them, and came to Nazareth; and He continued in subjection to them; and His mother treasured all these things in her heart. And Jesus kept increasing in wisdom and stature, and in favor with God and men." Luke 2:49, 51-52.

For Jesus, His relationship was in perfect balance with both the natural and the spiritual; His ongoing relationship with God the Father was priority in His life. This text tells us that he essentially grew in four ways as a result of His balance in this area: intellectually, physically, socially, and spiritually.

Jesus, (who was God manifested in His person and brought forth to show the only way to the Father), acts in love in weeping over the sins of Jerusalem in the passage of scripture at the beginning of this chapter. He says, *"How often I wanted to gather your children together, as a hen gathers her brood under her wings, and you would not have it!" Luke 13:34b.* As Jesus displayed in His ministry, he both honored women and his own mother, treating them with respect and admiration. He also displayed various qualities as a mother, showing compassion over people, being a healer of the their wounds, and acting many times in a mothering way to

A SPIRITUAL FATHER IS ONE WHO IS CONSTANTLY WITH THE FATHER

sustain His disciples. It is clear in this passage from Luke that He felt like a mother hen feels in gathering her chicks together to protect and bless, though He was rejected as God from many of His own children.

For Jesus, spending time in intimacy with Father provided the refreshing and recharging through which all "ministry" flowed out of. As God fashions and fits more of you to be spiritual fathers and mothers, keep this in mind. Cultivate your relationship as a son or daughter to The Father as the foundation for your ministry as a father or mother in the faith. "A spiritual father is one who is constantly with the Father, receiving revelation to pass on to others and to give," says Dorothy Langstaff, a mother in the faith and co-laborer with her husband, Alan, "but if he doesn't watch out he can fall into a trap and burn out. Any spiritual father must first be a son of the Father. He must always rest in the relationship he has being one of the sons of Father God. Our identity, even as spiritual fathers and mothers, must be that we are first and foremost children of the King, and our ministry flows out of our relationship with THE Father."

The Lord will turn the hearts of the fathers to their children, and the children to the fathers, both naturally and spiritually, so walk in this light and truth today.

"But Zion said, "The Lord has forsaken me, and the Lord has forgotten me. Can a woman forget her nursing child, and have no compassion on the son of her womb? Even these may forget, but I will not forget you. Behold, I have inscribed you on the palms of my hands; your walls are continually before Me." Isaiah 49:15-16.

Here is a beautiful piece of revelation from God. Since He contains "motherly traits" and He has passed on these traits to us as His children, we too can emanate such traits to each other, through the help of the Spirit. God utilizes the picture of a mother with her child, and the compassion that a mother feels for her child, to picture Himself like a mother who has compassion on her children. Zion here is the Church, (the church of which Jesus Christ is Head of and is pictured symbolically in the New Testament in several places as a Bride adorning herself for the wedding feast of the Lamb) and she is professing that perhaps God has forsaken her.

To many of the members of our generation, we are the lost boys and girls. Alienation from our families is one of the characteristics of our generation. There is so much that is twisted, unnatural, and out of order in family life today. The buzz word seems to be, "dysfunctional." Dysfunctional families fill the countryside and the city. And in the emerging young generation, nobody seems to know how to relate to each other in a normal fashion, much less to relate to God in a balanced way. Multitudes feel the same way this scripture passage relates, like, "Has God abandoned me? I don't feel love. I don't feel acceptance. I don't feel my needs are being met by God." And in a sense there's nothing new under the sun. Even the psalmist David felt this way, for he writes with hope and expectation.

"When you did say, "Seek My face," my heart said to You, "Your face, O Lord, will I seek." Do not hide your face from me, do not turn your servant away in anger; you have been my help; do not abandon me nor forsake me, O God of my salvation! For my father and my mother have forsaken me, but the Lord will take me up." Psalm 26:8-10.

This is one of the cries of our generation. We are fast becoming the generation of those who are radical lovers of God, since our own dads and moms have fallen so short in our lives. We are passionate about God, because only God can fill the deep need for companionship and nurturing and love and discipline we feel. We have had such a lack of godly training in some cases that we latch ahold of strong truth firmly, and though it hurts and exposes our weaknesses, we love the truth as a generation and need to hear and study it.

So the Lord responds to our cries with the mothering symbolism of ultimate caring and a sense that no matter how lost we may feel, the truth is, God will never leave us nor forsake us., and He has provide the church as our mother. The church, like God Himself, is the ultimate mother who can never forget her child. How infinite is the love of God! Human weakness may

HOW INFINITE IS THE LOVE OF GOD! HUMAN WEAKNESS MAY CAUSE NATURAL MOTHERS TO FORGET THEIR CHILDREN, BUT GOD WILL NEVER FORGET US.

cause natural mothers to forget their children, but God will never forget us. Matthew Henry's commentary fills in some deep understanding for this portion of scripture.

"*I have engravened you upon the palms of my hands.* This does not allude to the foolish art of palmistry, but to the custom of the day of those who tie a string upon their hands or fingers to put them in mind of things which they are afraid they shall forget, or to the wearing of signet-rings in remembrance of some dear friend. His setting them thus as a seal upon his arm denotes his setting them as a seal upon his heart, and his being ever mindful of them and their interests. *Your walls are continually before me.* That is, "Your walls (your safety) are my continual care; so are the watchmen on the walls. Some apply his engraving his church on the palms of his hands to the wounds in Christ's hands when he was crucified; he will look on the marks of them, and remember those for whom he suffered and died."[49]

The Church: About Father's Business, Performing Mother's Business

In the New Testament, the apostle Paul engages his readers and displays feeling the same feelings of a mother toward her children when he says to the church he had founded at Thessalonica, *"But we proved to be gentle among you, as a nursing mother tenderly cares for her own children." I Thessalonians 2:7.* Of course, to balance his leadership, he was also firm and disciplinary and sharp as relating to God as Father towards the churches he helped start, for in his next letter to the same group he says, *"And if anyone does not obey our instruction in this letter, take special note of that man and do not associate with him, so that he may be put to shame. And yet do not regard him as an enemy, but admonish him as a brother." II Thessalonians 3:14-15.* Hear how Paul lived in both a stance of soft love and hard love towards those whom he ministered to.

As a leader, learn from his example to give both to your flock. As a follower, learn to receive from God as father and from His church as mother, either directly or indirectly. Directly, from His relating to you through the power and ministry of the Holy Spirit. When Jesus spoke of the coming of the Spirit He said, *"And I will ask the Father, and He will give you another Helper, that he may be with you forever; that is, the Spirit of truth, whom the world cannot receive, because it does not behold Him or know Him, but you know Him because He abides with you, and will be in you. I will not leave you as orphans; I will come to you." John 14:16-18.* Hear the promise of Jesus to Generation X! He will not leave us as orphans! The disobedient children of Israel got His promises, but we obedient sons and daughters through faith in Christ get His presence! An abiding, ongoing, life-giving sense of God Himself as containing and giving both fatherly and motherly attributes a place within us. This is one of the great mysteries of our faith. Christ the supreme god-man, crucified for our weakness, raised from the dead for our justification, comes to us in the power of the Holy Spirit and we are no longer orphans on this earth!

We all share a common Father-God (with mothering instincts/attributes displayed through the Holy Spirit)! The Greek word for "helper" referring to the Holy Spirit is *paraclete*, or, "one called alongside to help." Remember our discussion about Eve, called the helper, and Yahweh, referred in the same Hebrew word in several places as helper? Now we have the ultimate fulfillment of the church as our mother. The

THE PRESENCE OF THE SPIRIT, RELEASED THROUGH THE "CALLED OUT ONES" AROUND US, IS OUR *PARACLETOS*

presence of the Spirit, released through the "called out ones" around us, is our *paracletos*. The imagery is taken from the time of the Greeks, when the armies would prepare themselves to go out to battle. They would host a parade, in their own honor, to encourage the troops as they went forth into war. People would gather alongside and be the "helpers" of the army, shouting out encouragements and showing support by coming alongside them. This is the same word for helper: *paraclete*. In the Amplified Bible this word carries with it a whole range of terms which display the character of God the Spirit and what the Spirit does for us: Counselor, Helper, Intercessor, Advocate, Strengthener, and Standby. So now the character of God is revealed in a revolutionary way, not just as Yahweh, but Paraclete.

THE PURPOSE FOR MANKIND: CHILDREN OF GOD

The final thoughts for this section center around the revelation that God has always desired to reveal Himself to His creation as a Father, Son and Spirit, with His church containing the fullness of His fathering and mothering characteristics. There is a scripture, a word which brings us back to the very beginning of time, which points to a time before time was created, before earth and man, which hints at this. It is found in Titus 1:1-3.

"Paul, a bondservant of God, and an apostle of Jesus Christ, for the faith of those chosen of God and the knowledge of the truth which is according to godliness, in the hope of eternal life, which God, who cannot lie, promised <u>long ages ago</u>, but at the proper time manifested, even His word, in the proclamation with which I was entrusted according to the commandment of God our Savior."

There is a beautiful promise in the middle of that verse. In the Greek, the word for "long ages ago" literally translated means, "before times eternal." In other words, to put it in layman's terms, before there was anything except the Father, Son, and Holy Spirit in existence, God's desire was to create a race of human beings on the earth who would have eternal life like He did. *"...in the hope of eternal life, which God, who cannot lie, promised before times eternal..."*

So God desired to create a race of personal beings who would love Him, and to whom He could pour out His love and give them eternal life. In Ephesians 1:5, the promise is similar: *"He predestined us to adoption as sons through Jesus Christ to Himself, according to the kind intention of His will."* Whose will? God the Father, for Paul writes in verse 3, *"Blessed be the God and Father of our Lord Jesus Christ..."*

So God was really after sonship/daughtership from the beginning of time itself. And His aim is the same for the end of time.

"He who overcomes shall inherit these things, and I will be His God, and he will be my son." Revelation 21:7. Did you ever notice here that God does not say "and I will be His Father?" He leaves it as "God" because we are sons and daughters of the Almighty, with God as our "father" and Christ's church as our "mother" for all eternity! The family atmosphere we encounter through the church on earth continues in the eternal realm!

You have become reconciled to God, and been made a minister of His reconciliation; you have been translated out of the realm of darkness in the kingdom of light; you have become an object of God's love, and the Holy Spirit Himself has been given to you, both internally and externally through Christ's church, with all of His glorious operations: He loves, disciplines, guides, gathers, protects, leads, and draws us to Himself.

An in-depth study of Romans 8 truly shows how the Holy Spirit leads us forward to true Sonship.

"For all who are being led by the Spirit of God, these are the sons of God. For you have not received a spirit of slavery leading to fear again, but you have received a spirit of adoption as sons by which we cry out, "Abba! Father!" The Spirit Himself bears witness with our spirit, that we are children of God, and if children, heirs also, heirs of God and fellow-heirs with Christ, if indeed we suffer with Him in order that we may also be glorified with Him." Romans 8:14-17.

In this passage you can hear the echo of Jesus' words that we looked at in previously about making us friends instead of slaves. We are in fact also adopted sons and daughters. He has not left us as orphans. The Spirit within us, (kind of like the mothering side of God), beckons us and reminds us that we are children of God. Back in the days of Hebrew child-rearing, the very first words that a baby was able to form were the simplest of syllables, for example, "Ab-ba." This is the intimate term for

"Da-ddy" or "Pa-pa" in today's language. We could also add "Ma-ma" here and be just as true to the meaning of the scripture. We are as little children to God! We are encouraged to come to Him and receive our spirit of sonship and daughtership by the Holy Spirit. Examine Galations 3 and 4 for further understanding of this great truth.

ABBA & MAMA

In conclusion, these two chapters were written to paint some broad brush-strokes of revelation of God and His awesome attributes which relate uniquely to our generation, and that as the Abba of all creation, He has chosen to reveal His characteristics to us for our development as sons and daughters in the church. I stand in line with historical theology and the doctrine

THE BROTHERS AND SISTERS AROUND YOU ARE HIS EXPRESSION OF YOUR TRUE MAMA IN YOUR OWN LIFE

and truth of the Trinity, and that God is known to us (through the revelation of Jesus mainly) as "He" and "Him" throughout scripture and that Jesus the perfect Son always referred to God as His and our 'Father'. Yet I wanted to give you a sense that especially for this current generation, many of whom have never experienced godly mothering or fathering, He is coming to us by His Spirit as both father and mother through the church.

The brothers and sisters around you are His expression of your true mama in your own life, if you will begin to relate to them as such.

His love is both soft and hard, and His truth as revealed throughout scripture transforms us. His discipline like a father and His compassion like a mother leads us to transformation. He disciplines us through the Spirit, through the living word, and through mentors and older Christians who have learned the hard way from their mistakes and desire to see the people they minister to walk in the ways of wisdom and freedom. For mentors, remember the revelation of this chapter, that through the ministry of the Holy Spirit, God is revealing His love, nurture, and character by the power He imparts. You can only point the way through your own maturity to Him, not take the place of the missing parent figures or seek to control or manipulate those who are coming into a knowledge of salvation. God is Father and His Spirit, by the ongoing ministry of Jesus Christ, brings the abiding presence to His children. Yield to His Spirit who will bring the very life of God, to those you minister to on a daily basis.

For now, let each of you learn to cultivate a friendship with God the Father and God the Son through the 'communion' of God the Holy Spirit in the context of Big Mama's House: the church. As a member of the Joshua Generation, let God's love for you become real: ask Him to pour it out to you and make it real.

In the following quote from the life of Howell Harris, be inspired by the line, *"I was drawn on by the love I had experienced."* Harris was a Generation X'er of his own day. He lived in the 1700's and was an uneducated Welsh man. At about the age of twenty he experienced a remarkable conversion and the love of the Father poured over him as if in waves. He then became the first preacher for hundreds of years in Wales to stand up in the streets and fields and proclaim Christ in the open-air. Both Wesley and Whitefield were inspired by the "forerunner" in their own ministries and as a result, set the world on fire by finding the freedom to proclaim Christ outside the boundaries of the walled churches of the day.

"A strong necessity was laid upon me," he wrote, "that I could not rest, but must go to the utmost of my ability to exhort. I could not meet or travel with anybody, rich or poor, young or old, without speaking to them concerning their souls...I was absolutely dark and ignorant with regard to the reasons of religion; I was drawn onwards by the love I had experienced, as a blind man was led, and therefore could not take notice of anything in the way. My food and my drink was praising my God. A fire was kindled in my spirit and I was clothed with power, and made altogether dead to earthly things...I lifted up my voice with authority, and fear and terror would be seen on all faces...I was given a commission to rend and break sinners in the most dreadful manner. I thundered greatly the mighty truths of the gospel."[50]

Of APPRENTICES
AND **MASTER MENTORS**
AROUND THE TABLE

*"Then the Lord said to Moses, 'Behold, the time for you
to die is near; call Joshua, and present yourselves at the
tent of meeting, that I may commission him.'"*

— Deuteronomy 31:14

CREATURES OF CHARACTER

"But the man of God must be..." Paul's first letter to Timothy

"Greenness is the test of a disciple. Is my path strewn with people whom I have touched into life? Worldly men can coerce others into conformity, but the man of God can ignite them into spontaneous, living obedience. But only—how important! if the disciple himself is in direct touch with Him who is life. Do the signs of life follow me—healed wounds, enlightened minds, neutralized self, reborn souls, purified relationships, contained evil, and an atmosphere charged with the glory of God?"

—anonymous

This final section of this book will address some issues relating to mentoring the next generation of radical apprentices and bringing them to the places in God they are meant to go.

In these last days, the Joshua's and Caleb's will be full of God, as they are the next generation of leaders and will be on fire for the Kingdom. The Moses generation will be full of expectation for training and releasing the Gen. X'ers around them. Spiritual qualities and strong Christian character must mark both generations.

The previous chapters laid forth the vision of God as "father" and the Church as "mother". There were a lot of things to say to both young men and young women, and older men and older women, who are equal in the eyes of God in terms of what each can experience in God and obtain in maturity. There remains then a structure of character to build on this foundation.

In essence, the qualities that mark both those called to lead and those who are being raised up to lead will be found complementing each other. Scripture tells us and shows us of many effectual qualities that become a part of our new nature in Christ as we walk on in maturity with Him. There are dozens of qualities which Paul lists in his letters to Titus and Timothy. Remember how we discussed discipline as an attribute of God the father/mother and His spiritual fathers/mothers of the faith? Let's also remember that we are called to live a life of discipline as well.

It is important to keep things in context. The first of three sections of this book dealt with casting vision; it was visionary in nature and should have you fired up as to the importance of the times and the part you have to play. We examined our current generation, its unique qualities, the spiritual battles that have shaped it, and cast vision as to this being a generation filled with the greatest possibilities since the Lord's creation of His Body on the earth. What Satan has meant for evil God will turn around for good. Now it's time to get practical. This section is dealing with ways to develop your life in God, giving you some practical examples and tips to become the warrior He has designed you to be, young or old. Joshua told the generation of warriors in front of him, *"Consecrate yourselves."* If you want to be a soldier, you must change your lifestyle!

FROM DISCIPLINE TO DISCIPLINES

We are not called to be hearers of the word only, but also doers. "Doers of the word" intimates that we take action to live a godly life. In most of Paul's epistles, he would first share with his audience the facts of who they were in Jesus Christ. Then he would share what they were to do because of who they were. Both are necessary and important. Godly discipline is one of the ancient landmarks to raise for this generation of undisciplined soldiers. One practical application you cannot escape from in these last days is instilling godly discipline into your life.

YOU NEED ONLY OBEY AND IMPLEMENT THE DISCIPLINES THAT YOUR SERGEANT OF THE GUARD TELLS YOU TO DO

Let's examine a few possible godly disciplines and see if you catch the vision to seek the Lord for more of them to implement in your life if you're not doing so already. Remember that in the Kingdom Jesus ushered in by His Holy Spirit, there are no set "rules" you are required to follow; no, you have a relationship with the King, and must only obey the promptings He places ever so gently within you. So as you read over this chapter, remember you don't need to copy what you read here to think you're being spiritual. You need only obey and implement the disciplines that your Sergeant of the Guard tells you to do. They may be different from the following ones, or the same. Read on!

First, do you have a special time and a special place to meet with God? Get one. Second, try to make it a point to read through the entire Bible at least twice a year as Martin Luther suggested. D.L. Moody gave further instruction on this discipline with Bible study when he said, "The Bible must first be read with a telescope, and then a microscope." In other words, read the broad books of the Bible and then go back for further study and really learn what some of those scriptures are saying.

EARLY TO BED, EARLY TO RISE

As a kid, I was required to be in bed every night at eight o'clock. I had to be up at a certain hour and be responsible to do my chores, get on the school bus, and all sorts of other things as I grew older.

It is the same way in our Christian walk. John Wesley used to plan his days in five-minute increments. His friend George Whitefield, (whom I wrote about earlier in this book) whose set hour to arise was four a.m., would retire by ten each night. Ever hear of Benjamin Franklin's statement, "Early to bed, early to rise, makes a man healthy, wealthy, and wise"? His life-long companion was Whitefield. I don't doubt that he coined that phrase from the testimony of his friend's life. Every evening, if Whitefield was in presence of others and it was his time to turn in, he would silently arise, walk towards the door, and say, "Gentlemen, it is time for all good men to be in bed."

Now, perhaps you've never made it a discipline of your Christian walk to have a set hour of arising. You might say, "That was fine for those men of God, but it's not for me." Well, need I remind you that it was said of Jesus Himself,

"And in the early morning, while it was still dark, He arose and went out and departed to a lonely place, and was praying there." Mark 1:35.

Now, I don't profess to be a Greek scholar; I usually say I know a little Greek and a little Hebrew; the Greek runs a restaurant and the Hebrew a clothing store! If you examine this text a little closer (excuse the pun), you'll find it is in the continuous tense in the Greek, meaning: *He practiced this continually*. It was a continual practice of Jesus to arise early and spend time in communion with Father. There is something special about arising early in the morning and spending time in communion with your God.

In the mid 19th Century, the students at Cambridge University in England became increasingly dissatisfied with their spiritual walks; they were continually busy with study, exams, and programs at the University. So they got together one morning and developed a program they called 'the morning watch' where

> IT WAS A CONTINUAL PRACTICE OF JESUS TO ARISE EARLY AND SPEND TIME IN COMMUNION WITH FATHER

every morning, regardless of the business of the coming day, they would spend time in fellowship with their God. The buzz word on campus between the godly students used to be, "remember the morning watch."

As you study the men and women of standard in the scriptures, you find that it repeatedly says of them that they "arose early in the morning." Make a commitment to begin to instill some godly discipline in your life.

Martin Luther once commented, "Work, work, work, from morning till night. In fact, I have so much work to do today that I shall need to spend three hours in prayer in the morning instead of two." Imagine! When his spiritual labors increased, instead of shrinking back in his commitment to intimacy with the Lord, Luther <u>increased</u> his time with God in the morning.

Of course, these next two scriptures are taken a bit out of context, but they seem to fit here!

"The night is almost gone, and the day is at hand. Let us therefore lay aside the deeds of darkness and put on the armor of light." Romans 13:12.

"Awake, sleeper, and rise from the dead, and Christ will shine on you." Ephesians 5:14.

John Wesley developed a list of disciplines and lived by them. Jonathan Edwards did the same; he had his "70 resolutions." A while back, I wrote down a list of fifteen that I could think of. Let me share them with you, not necessarily so that you will copy them, but to challenge you to develop some for your own life.

Standards for Life and Conduct, both long and short-term. Composed this seventh day of March, 1993. Carl Anderson, Jr.

1. Choose one day in every seven for rest, reflection, and inactivity. A Sabbath rest. Plan nothing. No ministry/telephone/appointments.

2. Eat lots of fruits and vegetables. Sugar but once every few days.

3. Take walk-study-breaks.

4. Carefully plan each hour.

5 . Be tidy, neat, and clean.

6. Keep heart strong. Exercise by running at least three times a week, twenty minutes minimum.

7. End each night by eleven p.m. and arise no later than seven a.m.

8. Take a nap each afternoon.

9. Drop all activities not directly related to your vision/preparation.

10. Be a giver—give generously.

11. Try to encourage at least one person every day and make their life brighter by the word of God.

12. Take one evening every week to spend with the Lord.

13. Memorize a new scripture every day.

14. Thank the Lord at the end of every day for His faithfulness.

15. Try to remember and practice these resolutions!

ORTHODOXY VS. FRUITFULNESS

In essence, in Jesus' own life and in ours, there were these two ingredients when it came to relating to the world: orthodoxy (or, living by precept) and fruitfulness (or, living by example).

Jesus went about, teaching the principles of the Kingdom, *"The Kingdom of God is like...a man who sowed good seed in the field; a mustard seed; leaven; tares and wheat; treasure hidden in the field; a pearl of great value; a dragnet cast into the sea, gathering fish..."* and then demonstrating them by example.

In your own life as a young or old soldier, there should be some system of order, or discipline, some aspect of being a "hearer of the word." To balance it, there should be some aspect of fruit, some demonstration of the kingdom, some portion of being a "doer of the word."

To put it another way, there should always be a balance

between truth and experience (like the previous peanut-butter-and-jelly sandwich example).

God did a powerful work of change through the early Reformers, but all that theological truth left a void in the church of God. So soon after He raised up a whole new group, called the Puritans, who took the truth of the early Reformation and brought the experience of daily application to it to make it real. We ARE this, and as a result, we LIVE like this.

Sadly, in too many church circles today, there is a mis-balance and the scales are tipped the other direction. Much theology is based upon having an experience with God; however, a proper understanding of the character and nature of God Himself is lacking as an undergirding foundation from which to base our experience. For example, we have already covered the foundational understanding of God as Father in the context of this arising last days ministry of the young. Many lack this proper foundation because their experience in growing up in a fatherless culture has warped their understanding of who God is and how awesome He is. Let's turn now to some character qualities that make a godly son or daughter and how to strive for them in your walk with God.

THE MARKS OF A SPIRITUAL SON/DAUGHTER

Again, whether you are young or old, male or female (for gender makes no difference in the family of God) there are certain marks, or characteristics, which God wants to stir up and fashion in you as His children in order for you to overcome the temptations which await us in the end days.

There are dozens of different character traits we could mention here. Since many other authors, including the Apostle Paul himself, have done a far more superior work in sharing them in different books or letters, let us examine only four. These four characteristics are crucial to your own formation in Christ's righteousness: teachability, humility, zeal and vision.

In the life of the Apostle Paul, these four qualities were almost forced upon him at an early part of his walk with Jesus. Like teachability for example. This great teacher of the law realized after his conversion that everything he had ever taught meant

SOMETIMES YOU HAVE TO UNLEARN THE OLD BEFORE YOU CAN INPUT AND LEARN THE NEW

nothing in comparison to the incomparable Christ. He spent an entire year at Antioch, fellowshipping with other brothers in the church and learning from them. We see him learning from other apostles like James in the church convention of Acts 15, and adapting his teachings and ways of ministry as a result. And he spent time in Tarsus, learning from working and preparing himself for a significant ministry. Sometimes you have to unlearn the old before you can input and learn the new.

As for humility, Paul's conversion and subsequent filling with the Holy Spirit three days later represent a great humbling experience; he was thrown off his horse, blind, fasted, and received the Holy Spirit through a common brother with no credentials! Throughout his life, humility was formed in him as well, as he later testified from his heart, *"whatever things which were gain to me, those things I have counted as loss for the sake of Christ."* *Philippians 3:7.* The striking thing about this particular verse is the

165

context. He had just listed all the things which normally any man in his position could be proud of. Yet to Paul, all was nothing that Christ may be found as all. He also was quoted as saying, *"to me, the very least of all saints, this grace was given."* Ephesians 3:8.

As to zeal, his own testimony of activity in the Book of Acts shows it as a common thread. He had such a fiery zeal to preach that even after in one city people rose up and stoned him with stones and left him as dead, he got up and went back in their faces to preach again! (see Acts 14:19-22). He also testified, *"woe is me if I preach not the gospel!"* I Corinthians 9:16.

As to vision, Paul was a man of vision from start to finish. He testified to the elders at Ephesus, *"But I do not consider my life of any account as dear to myself, in order that I may finish my course, and the ministry which I received from the Lord Jesus, to testify solemnly of the gospel of the grace of God."* Acts 20:24. He never lost sight of his vision. He knew what his course was and he was determined to follow it. Later he testified, *"Consequently, King Agrippa, I did not prove disobedient to the heavenly vision."* Acts 26:19. So Paul exhibited all four of these traits. Let's take a close look at each of them so you can begin to pray and ask the Holy Spirit to form them in your own walk and fashion you by experience to live with these as part of your character.

TEACHABILITY

One of the greatest attributes of a young man or woman of God is being teachable. Being teachable means staying open and as flexible as a new wineskin, for change, adaptability, and training and correction in righteousness. The key here is not to just listen to what others tell you about God; go to God Himself and learn of Him. It was Jesus who said, *"Come to Me, all who are weary and heavy laden, and I will give you rest."* Matthew 11:28. Incredible words, because no "god" up until the time of Christ had ever dared utter such personal words as these. The gods of the earth were powerful, sensual, and most important, impersonal. Here Jesus has the audacity to offer to anyone a personal relationship with Himself, inviting all who had open hearts and humble intentions to come to Him and receive true peace. Jesus was the most awesome "god" ever! No longer an impersonal relationship was needed. It was time for a change. This same beckoning from the heart of Jesus is in the earth today.

One of the amazing truths of the Apostle Paul's spiritual development was that he testified of a time in the desert, much like Moses had, where he learned from the Lord Himself; he purposely was not allowed to receive his training in Jerusalem, but went away so as not to adapt the habits of the flesh which were being adapted by the Jewish believers in Jerusalem and even the original Apostles. He explains that for a period of time in Damascus and Arabia he was taught of the Lord. No doubt his testimony in the first chapter of Galatians is vague for a purpose: he didn't need to reveal what he had been taught, only that the Lord had been his teacher. Paul was teachable. He was to be taught by the Lord Himself, and if you truly are teachable, the Holy Spirit will take you on as His chief pupil (or so He'll make you feel!) and teach you truth after truth. In fact, the apostle John encourages the first century church to do just that: let the Holy Spirit be a teacher. *"And as for you, the anointing which you received from Him abides in you, and you have no need for anyone to teach you; but as His anointing teaches you about all things, and is true and is not a lie, and just as it has taught you, you abide in Him."* I John 2:27.

Of course, there is a good combination needed of time with God where He Himself teaches you by the presence and power of the Holy Spirit and some friends around you who will teach you. A pastor friend of mine recently remarked to me that about

sixty percent of lessons and understanding come directly from
God, and the other forty percent comes from your relationships
to and friendships with fellow believers. The conversion of the
Apostle Paul was like this: Paul had intimate, personal revelation
directly from Jesus on the road to Damascus; he also had anoth-

60% OF LESSONS AND UNDERSTANDING COME DIRECTLY FROM GOD; 40% FROM RELATIONSHIPS AND FRIENDSHIPS

er piece of the pie of revelation given to him by an ordinary
believer of no known rank in the Kingdom. Together, the experiences taught him about Jesus and caused a great change in his
life.

HUMILITY

Here we will look at two sides of this multi-faceted quality
called humility. First, the posture, or outward quality. Every person of influence, be they younger or older, must develop an
approach to the world around them that views all potential people and situations as opportunities to learn something new. In so
doing, they posture themselves in an attitude of outward humility. Second, the inward quality. Every person of depth in the
Kingdom of God, be they young or old, has a commitment
within to humble themselves and to follow the course laid out
for them steadily, be it hard or easy, knowing that only God can
bring them through. First, the posture, or outward quality will

be explained (that is, how it plays itself out by your choice to abide in it).

"When you are invited by someone to a wedding feast, do not take the place of honor, lest someone more distinguished than you may have been invited by him, and he who invited you both shall come and say to you, 'Give place to this man,' and in disgrace you proceed to occupy the last place. But when you are invited, go and recline at the last place, so that when the one who has invited you comes, he may say to you, 'Friend, move up higher,' then you will have honor in the sight of all who are at the table with you. For everyone who exalts himself shall be humbled, and he who humbles himself shall be exalted." Luke 14:8-11. Jesus' audience to whom he spoke these words were people who desired only to cloak themselves in pride, to be well-known, and to draw attention only to themselves.

One day I had lunch with a friend and spiritual mentor of mine, Phil Buekler. He shared with me that when he was young and just getting into the ministry, he always tried to remain teachable and open, willing to change, and humble. This paid off for him one afternoon, as he had the opportunity to sit in the same room with some of the most well-known men of God of his day.

As the meeting progressed, he just listened, never opening up his mouth to make some comment or suggestion in order to "impress" these men of God. He just remained silent. Near the end of the discussion, one of them turned to him and asked, "What do you think?" It was then that he had a chance to share, but it was God who opened the door.

In Phil's mind he had something to learn from these men of God and the discussion. It never occurred to him to try and dominate the discussion because he was posturing himself in outward humility. Many times the strongest position is the neutral position. This means you are neither advancing or retreating in the situation, but simply remaining neutral and waiting on

God to open a door if He sees fit to do so. Can you see a link between these first two attributes, teachability and humility?

In the scripture passage quoted earlier from Matthew, Jesus teaches us to live in the opposite way of the world. Pride says, 'I am worthy of the seat of honor.' The flesh says, 'I take in rebellion what I am not offered.' Instead, the parable shows how the

MANY TIMES THE STRONGEST POSITION IS THE NEUTRAL POSITION

seat of honor should be reserved for the less fortunate, and the place of honor will be granted by God alone to the one who first takes the initiative to abase himself.

Another way of explaining the posture of outward humility is found in something I learned in a course I studied at Concordia College called, "Intercultural Communication," taught by my first mentor, Hank Tkachuk. It had both a theoretical aspect by teaching and discussions in a lecture hall and a practical one in a month-long study abroad program. The main theme of the whole course and experience is to take a neutral position in traveling to a new and diverse culture. In other words, instead of automatically assuming that the American way is "better" than the way something is done, you posture yourself in such a way as to put yourself in the shoes of the foreigner living in the foreign culture and try to see everything as they see it. Then you are swift to hear, slow to speak, and slow to make judgments or criticisms upon the people to whom you are visiting. "Our way" is not necessarily the "best way." It is simply the way we learned to do or say something.

Isn't this the posture that Jesus took? Jesus Christ, the God-man, who was equal with God throughout all eternity, long before the earth was created, emptied Himself of this honor, and laid aside this position of honor, to become like man. Paul writes about this in Phillipians, chapter 2. *"And being found in appearance as a man, He humbled Himself by becoming obedient." Phillipians 2:8a.* Interesting thought. Humility and obedience are the cornerstones of Christ's kingdom. The opposite of this is true in the satanic realm. For Satan, pride and rebellion are the cornerstones.

As a result of this revelation, you can be assured in your ministry that God will promote you when the timing is right. You can thus assume the lowly seat in many situations and watch how God will allow room to be made for your gift as you keep lowly in your heart.

The second quality of humility is inner humility, or the in-working of humility (that is, just what the Lord does with your heart and life over time to create a lowliness in you). True inward humility is seeing God for who He really is, and yourself as you really are, and then realizing that you can never live up to that comparison.

Recorded in Isaiah, chapter 6, is a remarkable incident of inward humility. In the first three verses, He has a vision of the Lord, and something of His character is revealed. It is a character marked with awesome holiness and the worldwide spread of His glory through His creation. Then in the light of that young Isaiah, probably about twenty years of age, sees his own helplessness. *"Woe is me,"* he exclaims, *"for I am ruined! Because I am a man of unclean lips, and live among a people of unclean lips, for my eyes have seen the King, the Lord of Hosts."* Humility is seeing yourself as truly undone, having no righteousness of your own in which to appear before God. Humility is seeing yourself as a beggar, looking for a few crumbs of the Bread of Life off the table of the Master, a sinner to whom God has bestowed mercy.

"Humility is perfect quietness of heart. It is to have no trouble. It is never to be fretted or vexed, or irritated, or sore, or disap-

HUMILITY...IS TO FEEL NOTHING DONE AGAINST ME

pointed; it is to expect nothing, to wonder at nothing that is done to me, to feel nothing done against me. It is to be at rest when I am blamed and despised. It is to have a blessed home in the Lord where I can go in and shut the door and kneel to my Father in secret, and be at peace, as in a deep sea of calmness when all around and above is trouble."[51]

The picture here is like a fish at the bottom of the raging sea. The peace that abides in a place like that is the peace that comes to your inner man as a result of humility being there. Isaiah knew that place, and that is why he was able to assume the duties and responsibilities of his office as a Prophet, and deliver messages which time after time caused his own countrymen to speak against him. He was able to roll all of his burdens, misunderstandings, and criticisms onto the Lord, and have faith that as the messenger His God would see him through. When storms raged around him, Isaiah was in a quiet calm of inner humility. *"And the work of righteousness will be peace, and the service of righteousness, quietness and confidence forever. Then my people will live in a peaceful habitation, and in secure dwellings and in undisturbed resting places; and it will hail when the forest comes down, and the city will be utterly laid low."* Isaiah 32: 17-19.

You can also rest assured that the deeper you grow in relationship with the Holy Spirit, the deeper He will draw you in the aspect of inner humility. He will especially guide you as it pertains to making godly choices each day. Jesus is our greatest example of this. He made a daily choice to bring His flesh in alignment with the Holy Spirit. He continually gave up His own rights to Himself in light of the Father's glory, and displaying the Father's glory. He expressed this in several different passages recorded in the gospel of John, translated and summarized as follows: *'I have no will of my own. I am committed to the Father's will first in all things. I do those things I see Him doing and my motivation is totally for His glory.'* On a daily basis, make a decision to surrender your heart in humility to Christ through the power of the Holy Spirit. Then a process will begin and will be carried on inside of you where you get into situations where the character faults inside you are exposed. Once exposed, God can deal with them, through your acts of confession and deciding to let Jesus crucify them on the cross afresh.

"The little faults become great and monstrous in our eyes as the pure light of God increases in us. Thus you see that the sun, as it rises, shows us the size of objects which we could only make out obscurely during the night. Remember that, as the inner light increases, you will see the imperfections which you have seen previously as basically much greater and more harmful than you had seen them up to the present. Moreover, you will see many other miseries, which you could never have expected to find, emerge in a crowd from your heart. You will find there all the weaknesses which you will need to lose confidence in your strength; but this experience, far from discouraging you, will help to uproot all your self-confidence, and to raze to the ground the whole edifice of pride. Nothing marks so much the solid advancement of a Christian person, as this view of his or her wretchedness without anxiety and without discouragement."[52]

It is interesting to note how this process of growth, challenge, dying to self, change, and maturity is symbolized throughout scripture. Sometimes the workings of the Holy Spirit planting faith and bringing God's people in maturity are pictured like the development of a tree or some aspect of a picture from nature, like the wind in John chapter 3.

One of the best examples throughout the New Testament is that of the development of a child. Peter's first letter and the writer of Hebrews uses this picture effectively. Faith is deposited in a person's spirit like the seed of life in the womb. Then comes the pregnancy and then the birth. Next the early development of the child of God, from infant to toddler to young man, where everything revolves around the "self" of the child, until that child is old enough to start making choices for good and not for evil. The child first needs to feed on milk to grow, and then later can handle meat. Finally as a child grows and assumes the responsibility as an adult so God delights when His children grow and live their lives before Him in perfect surrender and humility.

Humility is the mysterious quality of the heart which avails much growth throughout this part of the process. The words of the following poem aptly describe this process.

> "The world, I thought, belonged to me-
> Goods, gold and people, land and sea-
> Where'er I walked beneath God's sky
> In those old days my word was, "I."
>
> Years passed; there flashed my pathway near
> The fragment of a vision dear;
> My former word no more sufficed,
> And what I said was—"I and Christ."

But, O, the more I looked on Him,
His glory grew, while mine grew dim,
I shrank so small, He towered so high,
All I dared say was, "Christ and I."

Years more the vision held its place
And looked me steadily in the face;
I speak now in humbler tone,
And what I say is, 'Christ alone.'"

—*author unknown*

ZEAL

Zeal is the third attribute to consider working to obtain in your discipline as a member of the new generation of warriors currently being raised up. Zeal is a beautiful Divine attribute. It is a mighty energy-force. It is delivered from the heart of God into the heart of man and has as its outworking both excitement and surges of strength and warm desire to accomplish the works of God.

It was said of Martin Luther that he read and understood the scriptures more earnestly than any man had read them for a thousand years. English writer Iain Murray recently spoke at a conference and shared, "Zeal doesn't have its natural habitat in this world. It must come from Heaven. It is the temperature of the being, the fervor of earnestness, and a high degree of all the affections. Like varnish. Varnish is not one color in itself; but in the fire of the oven it gives gloss to all the colors. So zeal is spiritual heat in the heart." A commentator once said of English evangelist and reformer George Whitefield, "He was full of the love of God and fired with extraordinary zeal."

There are two great passages of scripture in the Old Testament which give us a glimpse of zeal, one in 2 Kings and one in

Isaiah. The first is the story of King Jehu. He was anointed king by a young prophet through the ministry of Elisha, and went forth with extraordinary purpose to bring to pass the word of the Lord in his generation. In chapters 9 and 10 you can read the whole story. In essence, he is a glitter of hope in his own time, being only one king who did what was right in the Northern Kingdom, referred to as Israel, over a period of 209 years and 19 different kings.

HE WAS FULL OF THE LOVE OF GOD AND FIRED WITH EXTRAORDINARY ZEAL

He acted in faith and set out immediately to fulfill the word of the Lord and destroy the wickedness of the house of Ahab. It was God's righteous judgment upon a wicked and evil people. Along the way, he meets up with Jehonadab, the son of Rechab, who was himself a righteous man. He greeted him by the road and said, *"Is your heart right, as my heart is with your heart?"* And Jehonadab answered, *"It is."* Jehu said, *"If it is, give me your hand."* And he took him up to him into the chariot. *And he said, "Come with me and see my zeal for the Lord."* So he made him ride in his chariot. He then commenced further judgment on the house of Ahab and destroyed all the worshippers of Baal in the land, and even turned their house of idolatrous worship into a toilet! Verse 28 says, *"Thus Jehu eradicated Baal out of Israel."* What was God's response to all this, after Jehu had acted in faith and with the character of zeal? *"And the Lord said to Jehu, "Because you have done well in executing what is right in My eyes, and have done to the house of Ahab according to all that was in My heart, your sons of the fourth generation shall sit on the throne of Israel."* II Kings 10:30. This is powerful! Zeal is an attribute of God, which flows from His heart to ours if we are seeking to do what is right in His eyes. The connection is clear: zeal is related directly to fulfilling the work and desire of God's heart. Let this be a challenge to the reader; seek God's face and cast away your own desires to embrace the plans that He puts in your heart. Then your heart will heat up with a spiritual fervency for the glory of God and zeal will be yours.

Let's look at a second passage in the Old Testament dealing with zeal. This one is related to Jesus Christ and His mission as the Son of God to carry out all the Father's good pleasure to His creation. It is found in Isaiah 59:17. *"And He put on righteousness like a breastplate, and a helmet of salvation on His head; and He put on garments of vengeance for clothing, and wrapped Himself with zeal as a mantle."* Here it pictures Christ as wearing zeal like a cloak. There is a fascinating story in John's gospel that relates the intense zeal He wore for His Father's glory. Let's take a look at it and see how the real Jesus, not always a meek little lamb, but sometimes a roaring lion of the tribe of Judah, displayed zeal, and then look at how you as a reader can wrap yourself in the same zeal as both Jehu and Jesus.

"And the Passover of the Jews was at hand, and Jesus went up to Jerusalem. And He found in the temple those who were selling oxen and sheep and doves, and the money-changers seated. And He made a scourge of cords, and drove them all out of the temple, with the sheep and the oxen; and He poured out the coins of the money-changers, and overturned their tables; and to those who were selling the doves He said, "Take these things away; stop making My Father's house a house of merchandise." His disciples remembered that it was written, "Zeal for Thy house will consume Me." John 2:15-17.

Why did Jesus have such a strong reaction here at the temple? The cause of this is found hidden in the Pentateuch of the scripture. Moses cries out with zeal in his heart in Deuteronomy:

"See, I have taught you statutes and judgments just as the Lord my God commanded me, that you should do thus in the land entering to possess it. So keep

and do them, for that is your wisdom and your understanding in the sight of the peoples who will hear all these statutes and say, 'Surely this great nation is a wise and understanding people.' "For what great nation is there that has a god so near to it as is the Lord our God whenever we call on Him." Deuteronomy 4:5-7.

Notice the context here is God's dealing with Israel to be a witness of Himself to the Gentiles, *"in the sight of the peoples."* His desire, right from the beginning, was to reveal Himself to Israel, and then have Israel in turn reveal Him to all the nations of the world. It was grace and truth in operation throughout the history of the old covenant. At first it was expressed with His law, itself an outward sign, which separated the ways of the people from all the other cultures to which they were being sent in the middle of. They would look and sound different than all the rest, and they would have a temple that would be different in design from all the other temples of the ancient world. Their temple, eventually built by Solomon, would have three distinct areas: an outer court (known as the court of the Gentiles since anyone of any nation could be welcomed there), an inner court (where the priests ministered to the people and performed sacrifices), and the Holy of Holies (where only the High Priest was allowed and the yearly sacrifice was made to atone for all the sins of the people, and where the mercy seat and His tangible presence was the light of the room).

So His desire and intent was to be a witness of light to the overshadowing darkness in the lands of the Gentiles, the foreigners from other bloodlines and nations besides the descendants of Abraham. Remarkably, this desire was made known from the heart of the Lord right from the beginning, even before they went in to conquer Canaan. Keep this context in mind and compare it with a text found in Isaiah 56, as Jesus quotes from it on that incredible day in the outer courts of the temple;

"Also the foreigners who join themselves to the Lord, to minister to Him, and to love the name of the Lord, to be His servants, every one who keeps from profaning the Sabbath, and holds fast My covenant; Even those I will bring to My holy mountain, and make them joyful in My house of prayer. Their burnt offerings and their sacrifices will be acceptable on My alter; for My house will be called a house of prayer for all peoples." Isaiah 56: 6-7.

God's plan had always been for the temple in Jerusalem to be a place where the glory of His revelation as God could reside. The outer court of the Temple, the only place the Gentiles were allowed to go, was meant from the beginning to be a place where His people were to interact with the foreigners. Here the saints and sinners could mix; the Gentiles could witness, if you will, their relationship with Jehovah. This would open up to the nations the truth of God, if perhaps even some of the Gentiles would reach out to find Him.

Now in the time of Christ, religion had caused the Outer Court to loose its witness. Instead of the Gentiles (or, "foreigners") being able to find God and understand more about Him, they found the merchandising of the gospel. Because of the sin and religiosity in the outer court, it became unclear to the Gentiles who Jehovah was. The witness to the nations was lost.

Jesus, perceiving this, grew zealous for the truth and purged and whipped; He fought for the truth with a zeal which did not abate.

What is the state of God's temple today? Look about yourself. See how religion and religiosity has caused the Gentiles, the world of the "foreigners", to grow cold and indifferent to the things of God. It's hard to detect who a true follower of The Way really is. The witness of Christ in so many lives has been distorted. The neutral meeting ground of the outer court is filled again with corruption. The word "Christian" is a slander and a stumbling-block to many people around the West.

179

Many in the world scorn believers, looking at them as a bunch of tithe-collecting, merchandise offering, hypocritical weaklings. Hollywood's perception of the church really brings this across. It's hard to find a good movie in the cinema where a believer is a good person, full of God's character and the fruit of the Spirit, and who does the right thing for the right motive. The reason? Too many in leadership have mixed too much of the world and the flesh and pride in their ministries, (in both Roman Catholic and Protestant traditions) and by doing have led many astray. The world is only acknowledging the Christ that they see represented. The fault lies squarely on our heads.

THE WORD, "CHRISTIAN" IS A SLANDER AND A STUMBLING-BLOCK TO MANY PEOPLE AROUND THE WEST

What is the answer for you to get the kind of zeal that motivated Jehu and Jesus Christ, or the early disciples to abandon everything familiar around them and go forth to be a true witness of God's love in the world? True zeal is a sovereign act from God's heart. You must get to a place of desperation and repentance. Repent and forsake the ways of your religious or non-religious past, and put yourself in the place of abandonment to God alone. Worship Him, fast, die to yourself and self-ambition, and let the warm breeze of zeal fire your heart. Meditate on the greatness of God and His glory and fashion a whip of leather. Wrap yourself in God's desires for this world like a cloak. The Amplified Bible clarifies the true definition of zeal from John 2:17. It reads, *"And his disciples remembered that it is written [in the Holy Scriptures], Zeal (the fervor of love) for Your house will eat Me up. [I will be consumed with jealousy for the honor of Your house.] [Psalm 69:9.]"*

Is it any wonder that James could write to the early believers, *"The Spirit Whom He has caused to dwell in us yearns over us and He yearns for the Spirit to be welcome with a jealous love?" James 4:5b.* God jealously desires you to walk in fellowship with Him by His Spirit, and the jealous love He has for the world will only be realized in a people set apart with an extraordinary zeal. A zeal which causes all your other desires except the honor of His house to be brought to the background in your heart. Let zeal burn within for the truth.

SPIRITUAL VISION

The final of four qualities being infused into the young genera-tion of Joshua and Caleb leaders and the Moses mentors in these days is spiritual vision. Spiritual vision is the ability to look beyond the circumstances you are currently a part of in order to catch hold and apprehend that which you see as God's plan. Having vision gives you the ability to impart to those around that which you see coming.

God often will take initiative with people whose hearts are His and share with them a word that enlarges their vision to some-thing greater. Growth and change are the earmarks of the Kingdom of God. One thing about us as believers: we are never the same after we receive Jesus Incarnate within us, and we are never the same until the day we go to be with Him. Paul said, "I press on..." and meant it. The believers' life with God is like an ever-changing river. Spiritual vision is what allows us to press ahead and prepare for the bends in the flow before they come.

The Lord often will ask us questions which allow us to look fur-ther than we are looking now. God wants us to relate to Him in the spiritual realm, and not so much the realm of the natural, in every area of our lives.

There is a great example of this and the kind of vision God wants us to have in Genesis 13. Two men have differing kinds of vision. One was Lot, and the other Abraham (known here as Abram, before the Lord changed his name). You can see the character difference between the two men in verses 4 and 5. Abram was a man whose heart was always seeking God for friendship, and Lot was more interested in just following the ways of God. Abram, *"called on the name of the Lord"* while Lot, *"went with Abram."* There is no record of Lot seeking God, only of Abram. Then because of some strife between their herdsmen, Abram decides to separate from Lot, and makes the decision to give him whatever land he desired. How could he do this? The answer is because he was walking with the vision God had given him earlier in the previous chapter. God had appeared to him and said, *"To your descendants I will give this land." Genesis 12:7b.*

So he knew in the spirit that somehow no matter what may happen in the natural, the bigger picture of all that land was that his descendants would possess it. Vision like this allowed him to make some short-term sacrifices, like not choosing the best land for himself. Instead he offered his nephew anything he

VISION LIKE THIS ALLOWED HIM TO MAKE SOME SHORT-TERM SACRIFICES

wanted. So verse 10 says, *"Lot lifted up his eyes and saw the valley of the Jordan—like the garden of the Lord."* He looked, not with spiritual vision, but with natural vision. He went by what his physical senses told him. Abram, being a man of true spiritual vision, saw differently. In verse 14 it says, *"And the Lord said to Abram, after Lot had separated from him, "Now lift up your eyes and look from the place where you are, northward and southward and eastward and westward; for all the land which you see, I will give it to you and to your descendants forever."* Wow! He lifted up his eyes, but he looked differently, in a different manner, than Lot. God let Lot choose what looked better in the natural, while allowing Abram to see with spiritual vision the true picture of all the land that was around him. Consequently, Abram moved forward and made wise plans to begin conquering what he knew was meant to be his.

Can you understand the difference, and how important it is to seek God for His vision for your life? This book is in itself meant to be a broad brush-stroke of a vision for God's unique plan for anyone born from 1960-2000 and how He's raising up a "yes!" generation, and a generation of mentors to bring them forward as a vast army. Within this broad vision, there is room for you. You have a unique purpose and part to play. The third section of this book is visionary in nature with more thoughts encouraging you to get that particular vision. But for now let God expand your understanding of seeing things the way He sees them.

According to Paul, *"Now we have received, not the spirit of the world, but the Spirit who is from God, that we might know the things freely given to us by God* (spiritual vison), *which things we also speak, not in words taught by human wisdom* (natural vision), *but in those taught by the Spirit, combining spiritual thoughts with spiritual words." I Corinthians* 2:12-13.
"While we look not at the things which are seen (natural vision), *but at the things which are not seen* (spiritual vision); *for the things which are seen are temporal, but the things which are not seen are eternal." II Corinthians* 4:18.

HE'S ON THE FIELD

The final section of this chapter will give some practical application for how to put into practice the disciplines which are in formation in your life. Character qualities such as teachability, humility, zeal, and spiritual vision are like electricity. The wiring is what the electrical current flows through. Different houses are wired in different ways, depending on the purpose for which the electricity is needed. Each person in the kingdom (and in the world) is essentially going to be wired from birth in one of three ways. I once heard a leader say that there are only three categories of people in the world. Remember as you read this that there is not one group better than the others; only different in nature and gifting and thus, calling. The three kinds of peo-

ABOUT 5% ARE INNOVATORS, 15% ARE ADAPTORS, AND 80% ARE ADOPTERS

ple are: innovators, adapters, and adopters. About 5% are innovators, 15% are adaptors, and about 80% are adopters.

Innovators are the people who blaze new trails; adaptors take the innovator's idea and adapt it to their particular situation; adopters take the smoother path of adopting what the adapters have put into place. And all three classes need the character quality of vision to bring about the work of God!

Think of the animal kingdom. The eagle is like the innovator. From his lofty heights, he is able to see far and wide that which is coming. If a storm is approaching, he can warn his fellow creatures and prepare ahead of time. The beaver is like the adaptor. He is continually building. Chopping down trees with his teeth, making his lodge, and swimming the lake in search of food to store up for winter are just a few ways he adapts the environment God has given him. The fish in the lakes are like the adopters. They just adopt their environment, and most of them swim in schools, following each other and living peacefully without concern for building big lodges, or for looking far ahead in the lake for storms or predators. Whether you're an eagle, a beaver, or a fish, you're valuable to God!

Think of an army about to fight a particular battle. The generals (the innovator-types) go ahead of everyone and figure out from their vast experience the bigger picture...where to place the guns, where to position for attack, and who will attack. Then the officers (the adapters-types) take the vision set before them and adapt it to their particular units under their command. They figure out some specific resources to fit the attack that the generals have laid out. Then the foot-soldiers (the adopters) strap on their boots, load their guns, muscle up courage, and charge. All of them combined doing their jobs mean success or failure for the battle. If everyone functions within their given sphere of authority and calling, then the battle can be won.

In the ancient records of Ireland, there was a saint named Brendan. He was a wild man. He was a part of an old monastery, and had an innovative kind of thought. Perhaps Ireland wasn't the end of the earth. Perhaps if he sailed far enough he would keep going to new lands. He gathered together a group of young men, and set out in his ship to discover a New World. His symbol was the wild goose, the old Celtic symbol for the Holy Spirit. The records of his journey lay buried for years in old books in a monastery. Five hundred years later, innovative Viking explorers would follow similar ideas and sail west in search of new lands. Five hundred years after the Vikings, a Portuguese explorer would begin to have thoughts that perhaps the world was round, and that if he sailed far enough toward the East, he would end up in Asia. He visited the old monastery records, and read there the journals of Saint Brendan. He saw some ancient maps from the Vikings, and probably read of their settlements in Greenland. He was an adapter. He adapted the innovations of Brendan and Viking leaders. Gaining money and able to outfit three ships, he sailed west. His name was Christopher Columbus. Another adapter followed closely in his footsteps, and discovered the coast of Florida. His name was Amerigo Vespucci. What followed were many Spanish and Portuguese pioneers, who arrived in this new world seeking to carve out a better life than the Old World offered. They were the adopters. So the innovators led the way, the adapters took the vision and set out to find the areas to settle, and the adopters settled and flourished.

The challenge in our day is to ask yourself, what category of person am I? How can I accomplish what God has put in my heart? Will everyone understand me?

Hear the words of Christopher Columbus' son, in the opening of the movie, <u>1492: Conquest of Paradise</u>. He shared, "Father used to say, 'Nothing that results from human progress is ever achieved with unanimous consent. And those who are enlightened before the others are condemned to pursue that light in spite of others.'" Whichever category of person you are currently, remember that possessing the qualities which this chapter discusses will help get you to the place where you can follow the path more firmly. Not everyone will always understand you in your calling as an innovator, an adopter, or an adapter. Go on anyway.

Whatever your part in the battle for the kingdom, the Holy Spirit is with you. He's somehow on all the parts of the field at the same time, directing the movements of the army and encouraging the hearts to be courageous. There is an old statement that goes something like this, "Form a habit, form a character; form a character, form a life."

Become a leader with teachability, humility, zeal, and vision, and take these character qualities with you as God forms His

THOSE WHO ARE ENLIGHTENED BEFORE THE OTHERS ARE CONDEMNED TO PURSUE THAT LIGHT IN SPITE OF OTHERS

life within you, whether it's a corn field (the place of growth of teachability and humility), a harvest field (where zeal is of the utmost importance), or a battlefield (where the ability to plan and fight with vision is central).

> "Oh, it is hard to work for God,
> To rise and take His part
> Upon this battle field of earth,
> And not sometimes lose heart!
>
> Ill masters good, good seems to change
> To ill with greatest ease;
> And, worst of all, the good with good
> Is at cross purposes.
>
> Workman of God! oh, lose not heart,
> But learn what God is like;
> And in the darkest battle-field
> You shall know where to strike.

Thrice blest is he to whom is given
The instinct that can tell
That God is on the field when He
Is most invisible.

Blest, too, is he who can divide
Where real right does lie,
And dares to take the side that seems
Wrong to man's blindfold eye.

For right is right, since God is God;
And right the day must win;
To doubt would be disloyalty,
To falter would be sin."

—F.W. Faber, from Quiet Hours, 1874.[53]

CHAPTER EIGHT

UNDER COVER

"And do not be called leaders, for One is your Leader, that is,
Christ. But the greatest among you shall be your servant."
Matthew 23:10-11.

"True greatness, true leadership, is achieved not by reducing men
to one's service but in giving oneself in selfless service to them."
–J. Oswald Sanders

Moses and his generation is called to help inspire the young
Joshuan cadets of Generation X who everywhere are
enlisting for service and preparing for the battles to come in the
decades ahead. In response to this, a proper understanding is
necessary for both young and old in the area of spiritual covering (this is one of the least understood and controversial subjects being addressed today).

On a recent trek through Europe, I paused in the chapel at
Schipol International Airport near Amsterdam and read a few of

the passages that folks had written at the logbook near the altar. A woman from California quoted this scripture passage:

"Behold, I am going to send you Elijah the prophet before the coming of the great and terrible day of the Lord. And he will restore the hearts of the fathers to their children, and the hearts of the children to their fathers, lest I come and smite the land with a curse." Malachi 4:5-6.

This is a powerful prophetic passage, and it deals with the end times. In one sense, it was applied to John the Baptist, who fulfilled it in preparing the way for the initial appearing of Jesus. Yet Jesus Himself hinted that it has not yet been fully realized. So there is coming a restoration, according to this scripture, of the hearts of the fathers to the children, and the children to the fathers. We can apply this in a couple of ways.

First, it can be viewed as having a more literal fulfillment: that in the last days, men will arise to be real men again. They will stand up for what is godly and true, and will be men of standard. They will take their rightful authority and stand in leadership positions in their homes, their families, their jobs, and their

MEN WILL ARISE AND BE REAL MEN AGAIN

churches. They will serve each other in humility and wisdom, and cause any wayward son or daughter to return and be bonded to them in godliness and sincerity.

There has been a movement in the 1990's throughout the United States called Promise Keepers. It was started by Coach

Bill McCartney in Boulder, Colorado, by a group of men who dedicated their lives to a closer walk with the Lord, and desired to see other men fulfill the same dedication. They filled football stadiums all over the country with men who were hungry and searching for something deeper to life. There was always an evangelistic message and altar call and many men came to the Lord. During these gatherings, teachings were given and then follow-up small groups were started challenging men to become men of standard in their communities.

Yet, in my estimation, one of the great prophetic applications for this movement was never properly addressed. The prophetic understanding of Malachi 4 to cause these men of standard to reach out cross-generationally and reach the young was never fulfilled in the movement. Of course, multitudes were inspired and encouraged. Yet if further such movements will make Malachi 4 a foundation, I believe they will exceed expectations. As was discussed in the first section of this book, the fields of the fatherless

MEN & WOMEN MUST RISE UP, IN BOTH THEIR STRENGTHS AND WEAKNESSES

must be harvested, and they can only be harvested by those disciplers and mentors who will stand up and be strong men (and women) of witness and commitment to the next generation.

Men must be men. Women must be women. Together, they can be mentors to great numbers of spiritual babies yet to be born, but which will some day outnumber the adults in the Kingdom. What a heritage!

Second, Malachi 4:6 has a spiritual application. God will cause a bonding and a unity between godly, spiritual fathers whom He is raising up, and children in the faith who need their hearts to be turned towards Him. If there has been no father in the home for you, there can be a father in the faith for you.

God's prophetic, spiritual purpose for Promise Keepers and similar movements among men, is to raise them up once again to be real men - men of standard, men of purpose, men who will take God at His word and live the truth for all to see. Men who will exemplify the character qualities mentioned in the previous chapter, and will become like fathers to spiritual children and uncles to spiritual nephews and nieces.

Men and women must rise up, in both their strengths and weaknesses, to prophetically *"turn the hearts of the children back to their fathers."* This will take people of all ages and backgrounds, who recognize the need to begin to pour their lives into others and see them raised up into the Kingdom; thus there is both a natural and spiritual application to the passage from Malachi.

CHILDREN, YOUNG MEN, AND FATHERS

Whoever you are, at whatever age or spiritual maturity, you undoubtedly fit into one of these three categories (these differ from the three categories at the end of the previous chapter in that they deal not with how someone is wired spiritually, but instead, the place where they are from a maturity standpoint). They are given to us by a man who went through all three phases of growth himself: the Apostle John. In I John we find him giving descriptions of all three categories.

"I am writing to you, little children, because your sins are forgiven you for His name's sake. I am writing to you, fathers, because you know Him who has been from the beginning. I am writing to you, young men, because you have overcome the evil one. I have written to you, children, because you know the Father. I have written to you, fathers, because you know Him who has been from the beginning. I have written to you, young men, because you are strong, and the word of God abides in you, and you have overcome the evil one." I John 2:12-14.

In essence, the children are those who are babes in Christ. They have come into the family of God, experienced forgiveness for their sins, and are beginning to learn how to walk. They stumble, as children do, and need others to lift them up.

The young men are those who have experienced something of the Lord. They know what it means to win a few victories. They are growing past the milk of the word (the fundamental elements and understandings of Christian experience) and they are developing their spiritual muscles.

The fathers are those who have come to experience THE Father. They are the smallest group, for they have come beyond just a relationship with Jesus. They aren't satisfied without being in the presence of the Father, and thus, it could be said that they bring the presence of the Father with them and carry it wherever they go.

A true spiritual leader will not just lecture a young apprentice; no, they will take that apprentice to the Lord in prayer and ask the Holy Spirit for a plan to help them mature and be led into a deeper walk with God Himself. In short, they will bring the very presence of the Father with them, and inspire the youth to passionately follow after and believe the truth of the Kingdom. Age is not a factor here; for spiritual fathers can be of any age, as long as they have been matured sufficiently by the Spirit and God has brought them to the place of Fatherhood.

RAISING THE LANDMARKS

Before we transition into a section on the topic of covering, it would be good to look at a practical way in which you can build a memory of God's faithfulness in your own life as a modern follower of Jesus.

In the ancient days, whenever an event happened which caused change in the life of a saint, they would build a marker or memorial there so that in generations to come both they, and their offspring, would remember the place. Spiritually speaking, the marker would help them remember the place in God where real, dramatic change took place and they altered their course to follow God more closely. This is an excellent and little-known spiritual practice for today. God desires that these types of spiritual landmarks be once again put into place as stepping-stones of faith for others to follow.

One practical way that the Lord still blesses thousands of years after it was first done is in building memorial stones to (1) remind ourselves of past victories and (2) remind those who will follow of the Lord's faithfulness.

One example of this was in the book of Joshua, just after all the children of Israel crossed over the Jordan. God spoke to Joshua and commanded him to take twelve stones, one representing each tribe, and set them up as a memorial for their children after them, to teach and train them. It was a physical manifestation which represented a spiritual deliverance and truth, so that indeed *"all the peoples of the earth may know that the Lord is mighty"* (*Joshua 4:19-24*). As the Moses generation, do you have any physical reminders in your life to help train the next generation in the faithfulness of the Lord? As the Joshua/Caleb generation, have you set up special markers along the way to remind yourselves of God's faithfulness?

Often as a young cadet, God would be continually changing me, and showing me areas of repentance in my heart. I would respond to altar calls with tears, and real transformation would happen. Sometimes I would go out and purchase little reminders of the place of repentance I had made in God, like a little cross or other jewelry to wear. Once I even bought a red bandana which I occasionally wore around my neck to remind myself that God had called me as a young pioneer!

OFTEN AS A YOUNG CADET, GOD WOULD BE CONTINUALLY CHANGING ME, AND SHOWING ME AREAS OF REPENTANCE IN MY HEART

I remember a great battle I went through to purchase my first house. During the process, lots of money had been saved up for the down payment, and all seemed well, until toward the last week of the closing the bank decided to investigate me further and postponed the closing. I went to prayer, and during worship the Lord spoke to my heart. "The house is yours." In the natural, lots of obstacles still lay in the way of the fulfillment of that word, yet in my heart I knew that God had given the victory. "Go to the mall," He said to me, "and purchase a Thomas Kincaid painting. Spend as much as you need to get the one you want. Then when you get the house, put it up in a prominent place for all to see, and as a reminder of My faithfulness to you." So I shared this with my wife, and off to the mall we went. We got the house, and that picture still stands as a silent reminder to the God who delivered us and will always deliver us in His faithfulness in the coming days.

THE TRUTH ABOUT COVERING

It follows, after understanding true fathering and mothering, and being inspired to pass along to others the good in what we are learning from following Jesus, that the subject of covering should be addressed. My aim is to show first what godly covering is, and give some examples of it, and then to share what it is not. I've personally had some instances of both good and bad examples in my walk with the Lord, and the negative experiences could have been altered if both parties involved would have had a clearer picture from the scriptures about covering and the question of authority and individual direction in Christian leadership. Let me begin by the good qualities of covering as it relates to leadership in our Generation X context, for all of us in some measure are, 'under cover' operatives in the Kingdom!

A dear intercessor friend was recently in prayer and asked the Lord about the whole subject of covering. When she went to the Bible to find references, she found almost none. So the Lord asked her a question.

"Who covered the children of Israel?"

"You did, Lord."

"And how did I do this?"

"Well, by the cloud by day and the pillar of fire by night, Lord."

"Exactly. My glory was my covering."

So, the Lord is revealing here that in Old Testament days His glory was His only covering; the cloud of the Lord's presence brought the people the proper safety and direction they needed. You can read about it in the whole chapter of Number 11. God

Himself showed Himself responsible for their well-being and safe-keeping. By day the cloud offered cool protection from the hot desert sun, and by night the appearance of fire offered both light and heat from the cool nights in the desert. His glory covered them and brought safety and protection.

In New Testament understanding, we could say that the blood of Jesus Christ is the first and foremost covering that we have.

"For by one offering He has perfected for all time those who are being sanctified. Since therefore, brethren, we have confidence to enter the holy place by the blood of Jesus, by a new and living way which He inaugurated for us through the veil, that is, His flesh, and since we have a great priest over the house of God, let us draw near with a sincere heart in full assurance of faith, having our hearts sprinkled clean from an evil conscience and our bodies washed with pure water." Hebrews 10:14,19-22.

Here in this passage, God makes it quite clear that by Jesus' sacrifice, He has become the great priest over the house of God.

THE BLOOD OF JESUS CHRIST IS THE FIRST AND FOREMOST COVERING THAT WE HAVE

We need only walk in the confession of the covering of the blood of Jesus to have the instantaneous, most powerful covering in the universe.

In defining this subject, we take as our definition that covering is from God the Father alone through the atonement of Jesus Christ, and thus not only protection and direction, but also in a sense a responsibility to pay the price for sinful or wrong choices. It is this third aspect that is never taught and is rarely understood. You see, when the Father sent Jesus to the cross to pay the price for sin, He was in essence taking personal responsibility for the wicked, unholy sin-nature of all mankind. In short, your sin placed Jesus on the cross, and God judged it with the death of Christ.

He took responsibility for your actions; this is a supreme aspect of covering to comprehend. For example, a father whose son throws a baseball into the neighbor's window will act as the rep-

YOUR SIN PLACED JESUS ON THE CROSS, AND GOD JUDGED IT WITH THE DEATH OF CHRIST

resentative of godly authority over his son in dealing with the issue; he will approach the neighbor with this in mind, take responsibility for the son's actions, and offer to pay for the cost of the broken window as the son cannot afford such a price.

The commandments of God being broken from our birth, the price of our sin is too great for us to pay. The shedding of blood for forgiveness and the sentence of death is the only price great enough to pay; so God steps in with His covering and Jesus' blood paves the way. We are set free by the authority of the Father in our life.

Another example might be the general of an army, whose chief officer is caught in a scandal, but who steps down as a result and resigns, for the officer in his care committed wrong and he assumes responsibility for the sinful wrongdoing of the one under his command. So our heavenly Father shows us the way to act as both being under His covering and then providing oversight to others under the same covering as us.

This is the meaning of the later words of Hebrews:

"Obey your spiritual leaders and submit to them; for they keep watch over your souls, as those who will give an account." Hebrews 13:17.

The early church recognized the truth of leadership in the body, that there are those called to keep you safe and pray for your advancement in spiritual maturity; and these elders and leaders are ultimately held accountable before God to how well they execute this job.

The fields of the fatherless are strewn with sons and daughters who despise true authority, and as they are brought forth into the Kingdom, the last thing they need is for a wrong understanding of authority in the government of God's Kingdom, which is why it is necessary to address it in this chapter.

Ultimately, each and every person reading this book who is a member of the household of God is responsible to only One: the King Himself. God is your ultimate source and your ultimate aim; unto the leading of His Spirit are you held accountable both daily and on the day of Judgment.

That being understood, how then do we walk out a pure walk before God? For it is a narrow road, and many a good-hearted saint has started out right only to end up a Lone Ranger, and be dismounted in a ditch somewhere with a dead horse and a broken canteen.

Take that scripture in Hebrews with this in mind: God sets in every life a set of friends/spiritual counselors to whom they can look for accountability and prayer purposes in making godly decisions. There is a special net, if you will, of a handful of relationships in every life designed by God to be prayer partners and independent counselors to provide godly, righteous covering and direction ordained by the Holy Spirit. These people are not in your life to control you; they are there to pray and offer counsel when asked so that you can make the proper decisions and follow The Way even better. This is the burning truth for this hour! This is how you mature!

Perhaps you've read the scriptures from Proverbs,

"Where there is no guidance, the people fall, but in abundance of counselors there is victory." and again, *"The way of a fool is right in his own eyes, but a wise man is he who listens to counsel."* and yet again, *"Without consultation, plans are frustrated, but with many counselors they succeed."* Proverbs 11:14, 12:15, 15:22.

Take these passages in this special light of truth, if you're mature enough to accept it. The multitude of counselors Proverbs speaks of are those nets of relationships God has ordained in your life to pray and discern His voice for you, and offer to you the wisdom of the Spirit regarding situations and choices you

THE **MULTITUDE** OF **COUNSELORS PROVERBS SPEAKS** OF **ARE THOSE NETS** OF **RELATIONSHIPS GOD** HAS **ORDAINED IN YOUR LIFE TO PRAY AND DISCERN HIS VOICE FOR YOU** must make. This counsel is offered separately by these circles of friends, and as you take it and pray about it, you compare it with the Holy Spirit's voice and then make your decisions independently under this web of godly covering. You still have the element of faith involved in every step you take. It's just that you now have added confirmation about a "yes" or a "no" in certain directions or areas. If the leader of your church or your spiritual mentor happens to be one of these people that you select, you will be doubly blessed, as it will honor them to know that you consider them of deep discernment to ask them to pray for you and help you make decisions, and you will be blessed by honoring those among you who hold such offices.

DIRECTION, NOT DICTATION

Now let's address what is not godly covering, as there is so much taught and practiced these days that carries with it abuse of this subject. This section is especially addressed to those who have been placed in spiritual leadership by the Lord Jesus to help govern aspects of His Kingdom on earth.

The question becomes one of authority. Here are some negative things that I have heard in certain past church leadership experiences. "You have to be under authority, you have to submit to my pastoral leadership, you have to obey me, you must be accountable to me." There is a huge false doctrine alive and well in certain churches today which states that Christians must submit to their pastors. And "submit" usually means, "control." Let's face it, it's a much easier path to go the way of the flesh once someone reaches a place of leadership, and tries to square responsibility for his flock with natural ability.

An incredible film which shows this stars Michael Caine and Sean Connery called, "The Man Who Would Be King." In it, these two men who are imposters get accepted as royalty to a certain tribe and one of them, because of the money and power afforded him, turns on the other, ultimately costing him his friendship and his life. Many in leadership today would learn a good lesson in watching this film and then repenting of any tendencies in their own hearts of seeking to lord authority over those whom they are called by God to properly oversee. It's a much harder course to assume the posture of Jesus Christ, who said, *"I came not to be served, but to serve, that I might give my life a ransom for many." Matthew 20:28.* We could make a film about Jesus Christ's or the Apostle Paul's leadership styles and call it, "The Man Who Would Be Servant."

It takes a special kind of leader to recognize their place in partial covering is to discern the gifts of the young around them and help them develop those gifts for God's glory, and then release them with vision to fly higher than they did. "There are two things we can give our children," said Alan Langstaff to me one day, "one is roots, and the other is wings." Harry S. Truman put it this way, "I have found the best way to give advice to your children is to find out what they want and then advise them to do it." Mentors need to help direct the flock, not dictate or rule.

I remember sitting and speaking to a mentor in the faith, one of the elders of the congregation I was attending. I had just made some mistakes in ministry, and felt bad about them. He came and sat next to me.

"It seems to me," he said, warmly, "that when God is preparing His men to be moved up in rank in His army rather quickly, He deals rather harshly with them at the same time."

He made me feel love and also discipline at the same time yet with God's greater vision that the season I was in was actually leading somewhere. Here was a wise way to bring correction and direction at the same time.

There is some solid scriptural evidence that God gives elders in local congregations certain authority to pray and watch over those people they are called to serve, but the truth about the subject is that no person in the true Kingdom has "authority" over any other person to rule over them. Remember earlier in the book where I shared that in the garden of Eden, the Lord gave Adam and all mankind authority over almost everything in the whole realm of earth, except one thing: other men. The one possible exception to this rule being the husband-wife relationship where God has placed His mantle of responsibility on the husband to administer the affairs of his household showing forth the Father's authority. For a fuller scriptural explanation of this part of the subject in regards to the husband-wife relationship, please read I Corinthians 11:3 and Ephesians 5:22-33.

THOSE WHO ARE CALLED IN FIVE-FOLD OFFICES ARE MEANT TO BE THE GREATEST SERVANTS OF ALL, SINCE THEIR WORK IS TO WORK THEMSELVES OUT OF A JOB

One of the ways that many in the Body of Christ in leadership are changing these days to come more full-circle in understanding their calling as "coaches" and not "dictators" is found in Ephesians 4. There, Paul mentions that those who are called in five-fold offices like apostles and pastors and so forth are meant to be the greatest servants of all, since their work is to work themselves out of a job. In other words, their work is for, *"the equipping of the saints for the work of service." Ephesians 4:12a.* Often, a leader simply needs to have the courage and step out of the way to give a younger person an opportunity for advancement or even to allow them to make a mistake in their own direction for life. The bottom line on covering from a leadership perspective is for the leader to recognize the difference between <u>government</u> in Jesus' kingdom and <u>inspired direction</u> from the Holy Spirit. The key may be simply to recognize how you've mixed up these two in the past, repent for your error, and then get a fresh start in letting the Spirit take that place of direction and allow the apprentices under your watch to make their own decisions for a change.

OUR IN-HOUSE SECURITY SYSTEM

If you are reading this book as a young soldier, learn this truth right now: no other person in the Kingdom has the right to control your walk or dictate the way in which you should live, for there is only one true "covering" and He is Jesus Christ. His blood is the true covering for you, and His word and Spirit are meant to be your guidance and direction. Remember that passage of scripture from Hebrews chapter ten? The blood of Jesus is a new and living way, and all who stand under that covering can have a sincere heart and full assurance of faith. Did any pastor or mentor die and shed his blood for you? A ridiculous thought at best! So it is just as ridiculous for a man who himself is in a place of some authority and spiritual maturity to make you submit to him, as if the blood of Jesus was not enough.

I have had instances where the pastor or leader I was working with didn't even have the time to pray for me and really discern God's voice for me. They simply wielded the rod of their authority (which I had voluntarily given them hoping for them to use it carefully and not abuse it) and would tell me "yes" or "no" to certain things without the fresh direction or input from the Holy Spirit. This left me confused and sometimes hurt and occasionally brought a breach in our relationship. If we both had had this fuller understanding of the subject, we would have been in a win-win situation every time.

Of course, I am not addressing here the subjects of constructive criticism, behavioral changes in character, and church discipline. Only the matter of covering as it relates to authority and direction. This chapter is meant to encourage all believers in the Lord that they're accountable ultimately only to the Father through Jesus Christ and are covered by His blood and protected by the Holy Spirit, but that the Body of Christ has its own in-house security system: relationships with discernment and love to help you on your way!

> "Because we children of Adam want to become great,
>   He became small.
> Because we will not stoop,
>   He humbled Himself.
> Because we want to rule,
>   He came to serve."
>
> *—anonymous*

THE MENTOR OF MONTE CHRISTO

"There is a deep spiritual significance, a plus factor that this generation can bring. But they need mentoring." –Phil Buekler

"When the pupil is ready, the master shall appear." –Zorro, quoting an ancient saying to his young apprentice, from a recent re-make of the film starring Anthony Hopkins as the Mentor to a new generation of Zorros.

In this chapter the call for spiritual mentors to rise up and be counted will be practically addressed, along with some tips for the younger generation to seek special relationships with mentors and receive special instruction for their lives. The Holy Spirit Himself trains and equips us, though mentors are needed to spur us on to growth and maturity.

Those who are master-swordsmen and women need to catch the vision of the young apprentices around them and begin to train them in technique and commission them to fight the giants in the land.

APPRENTICE LEADS TO JEDI KNIGHT; JEDI KNIGHT LEADS TO JEDI MASTER

Everyone of my generation recognizes Star Wars. The original film was released when I was just seven years old, in 1977. Luke Skywalker gets apprenticed by Obi Wan, and soon becomes a Jedi Knight himself, surpassing the level of Obi Wan at a much younger age, through the help and training of Yoda, which was the progression into the second film of the trilogy. Later in the next film he becomes a Jedi Master, and faces the biggest battle of his life: fighting Darth Vader, who in an ironic twist turns out to be his own father. These films point to a wonderful picture of God's design for Generation X to be brought from boyhood stage, or apprentice stage, to full mentored and released stage

WHAT IS ONE OF THE KEYS TO RELEASING OUR GENERATION OF KNIGHTS AND FAIR MAIDENS? THE ANSWER IS: APPRENTICESHIP

(the Jedi Masters of God's Kingdom)! Of course, to be true to God's ways, George Lucas had better figure out that the next film after Return of the Jedi should center around Luke training other Jedi Knights and having apprenticeship relationships with them!

The theme for this chapter is the theme of practical training, or mentoring. Some of this book is theoretical, some theological, some inspirational, and this section will be more practical. What is one of the keys to releasing our generation of knights and fair maidens? The answer is: apprenticeship, which can be defined as the process of relationship between two parties, one of them older and experienced, and one of them younger and inexperienced, to bring the younger to their next step of maturity in God, and release the older to grow even further in his/her ministry.

I will break this down under the thematic heading of mentoring and share on three separate categories: indirect apprenticeship, direct apprenticeship, and coaching.

INDIRECT APPRENTICESHIP

First, what has been termed in some circles as indirect apprenticeship. Indirect apprenticeship is where the Lord is involved in the background of the training, but the person being trained is working indirectly with the Holy Spirit Himself and directly with a human being (the mentor). You can see many examples of this method in the scriptures. Our greatest example in this book is Moses and his relationship to Joshua. Joshua accompanied Moses up and down the mountain, in and out of the tents of meeting, around the camp, and probably got under his skin more than a few times (but since his skin was glowing with God's presence I'm sure he didn't mind it very much). Joshua's training was in the presence of Moses, and Moses accepted the responsibility firmly on his shoulders. Ultimately, God asked Moses to lay his hands on Joshua and commission him to be the chosen leader to succeed him and release him in his ministry.

Other examples in scripture of indirect apprenticeship are the relationship of Elijah the prophet with Elisha, and in the New Testament of the relationship between Paul and Timothy or Barnabus and Mark. In each case, they would travel together and the older would take interest and train the younger in the ways of the Spirit. The main truth that the Lord revealed in each case was that He spent a good number of years in each of the lives to purge out the natural tendencies to do things their own way, and birthed in them a strong sense of learning to be led by the Holy Spirit, either internally or externally. In short, the process caused them to unlearn man's ways and learn God's ways, which are usually quite different.

Notice something: in each case mentioned above, the calling and subsequent ministry of each of the apprentices was often both different and went to another level in the next generation. Joshua arose and took the land that Moses was forbidden to step foot in; Elisha arose with a double-portion anointing than his predecessor; and Timothy became a voice and translator of much of the truths that Paul learned from the Holy Spirit, and no doubt spread the ministry of the Spirit throughout the many churches in the world which had been opened to both Jews and Gentiles. *"And the things which you have heard from me in the presence of many witnesses, these entrust to faithful men, who will be able to teach others also."* II Timothy 2:2. In our Star Wars example, you can trace how Luke was working with Obi Wan and later with Yoda in this indirect form of apprenticing.

DIRECT APPRENTICESHIP

The second form of mentoring is called direct apprenticeship. Here, the Lord Himself is doing the mentoring, and another party is not so directly involved in the process. This is the hardest to explain, because in one sense there isn't much written about it, and God's ways are higher than man's, and he handles each individual case a bit differently. God will move His children in and out of seasons of direct apprenticeship to accomplish character building where no one relationship or one set of circumstances can be traced to be the central means.

Moses is one example of having been mentored like this, in the ways the Lord led him in the wilderness for forty years. You might say that Jethro, his father-in-law whom he worked for during those years in the wilderness was the mentor, or that his wife was the mentor, or that working with his own hands was the mentor, or that he learned God's ways through nature around him and that was the mentor (enough for him to stop and know that a burning bush was supernatural and he'd better take a closer look)!

You would be correct to say that all these and other events and people that made up his forty years in the back side of the

GOD USED EVERYTHING IN MOSES' LIFE TO SECRETLY TEACH HIM LESSONS

desert were the mentors, yet in one sense it was only God Himself who was, and he used everything in Moses' life to secretly teach him lessons, because his heart was willing. No one of any of these people were directly mentoring him, and yet he learned many things about God and unlearned many bad habits and Egyptian traditions through the circumstances God allowed during those years. It's almost like God goes ahead of the apprentice, sees down the road who that person needs to meet and when, what circumstances brought to bear would be the best to teach and train, and then secretly and mysteriously sets everything in motion so that it all works out by the free will choice of the apprentice and other significant relationships just the way it was supposed to.

Other cases of direct mentoring would be John the Baptist, who spent many years alone in his one desert experience, or the Apostle Paul, who spent twelve years being taught of Jesus both in Arabia and working in Tarsus before beginning his ministry in Antioch. In the third Star Wars film of the trilogy, a case could be made that God was directly mentoring Luke through the internal struggles he had to deal with once he discovered that the evil Darth Vader was in fact his father and once a good Jedi Knight like himself. He learned ultimately not only forgiveness but helped his own father redeem himself in turning back to the side of the truth and destroying the emperor.

CALLING ALL COACHES

The third form of mentoring is called coaching. Coaching is taking an active form of relationship between the person experienced in a particular ministry and the person called in a particular area. Coaching is meant to be for a specific purpose of improvement and for a specific season of time. Of course, a true mentor is one who learns how to coach others, offering help, advice, spiritual wisdom, and godly council, but who leaves the actual playing of the game to the team. Yet coaching as its own form of apprenticeship is effective in that it is encouraging and for a specific skill to be developed. A coach may be someone skilled in intercession for example, hearing other people pray and then helping them to pray better. Or the same could be true in preaching or teaching, or church administration work, or spiritual gifts and their development in the life of a believer.

One great example of coaching is found in Acts. *"Now a certain Jew named Apollos, an Alexandrian by birth, an eloquent man, came to*

Ephesus; and he was mighty in the scriptures. This man had been instructed in the way of the Lord; and being fervent in spirit, he was speaking and teaching accurately the things concerning Jesus, being acquainted only with the baptism of John; and he began to speak out boldly in the synagogue. But when Priscilla and Aquila heard him, they took him aside and explained to him the way of God more accurately." Acts 18:24-26. Can you see how Priscilla and Aquila were coaches? They encouraged an already dynamic leader to become even more dynamic. He goes on to

THEY ENCOURAGED AN ALREADY DYNAMIC LEADER TO BECOME EVEN MORE DYNAMIC. HE GOES ON TO MAKE AN EVEN BIGGER IMPACT IN MINISTRY

make an even bigger impact in his ministry, as recorded in the next few verses, as a result of this encounter of coaching. In the Star Wars films, Luke Skywalker was coached in how to shoot better by his buddy Han Solo, and was coached in public relations by his sister, Princess Leah.

I remember one year after I had graduated from Bible college and had a couple years of itinerant evangelism under my belt, the pastor of my local church, Alan Langstaff, who was also an effective mentor, sat down with me after praying and offered me a staff pastor position as an intern. He had prayed about it, and knowing my character strengths and weaknesses ahead of time, offered a specific description of duties which wouldn't put a cramp on my calling to the nations but which would ultimately bring more balance to me as a young minister. It had a specific time-frame of one year, a set of boundaries and tasks, and a good amount of slave labor attached! He ended it with the phrase, "ashes to ashes, dust to dust, what the pastor won't do, the assistant must." This was both an example of indirect mentoring and coaching.

Then a few years later you could say I underwent a direct-mentoring approach from God Himself. He saw that at age 26 I was too full of pride and still wanting the praise of men rather than the praise of God, and offered me a forced retirement from all ministry. In fact, I died to all vision and all active ministry for a period of nearly four years, during which time I got married, started working in forming my own video business, and started a family. Along the way, lots of character issues got addressed and then came the re-establishment of my calling to impact the world for Christ. God the Father acted as a silent and secretive mentor this whole time.

A coach should develop a strategy with those they are mentoring. A good strategy will allow for five main areas. First, both failure and growth for the apprentice will be designed. Second, a way to confirm the apprentice's calling to leadership, hopefully in the presence of others, will be addressed. Third, it will expose and remedy fundamental character flaws, and give room for positive recovery when issues come up. Fourth, it will be relational in nature, giving the necessary time to the relationship and sacrificing other things for a season to see the apprentice grow. Fifth and finally, it will recognize when the coaches' role is complete and the apprentice can be released. A specific "context" may be drawn up with a realistic timeframe and responsibilities on both mentor and apprentice attached and signed by both parties.

DISCIPLE BECOMES DISCIPLER

Much can be said here about the process Jesus taught us in apprenticeship. It is enough to relate that though Jesus walked the earth, fed and healed thousands of people, in a few years his earthly ministry would have been forgotten, had it not been for the twelve men He took with Him to reproduce that which He had done.

The most amazing part about the book of Acts is that it is the only book ever written about a man whose greatest works were done after He was dead. Did you ever think about that? Of course, Jesus rose again and had already ascended into heaven when the miraculous began in the lives of His disciples through the power of the Holy Spirit.

He was doing these works <u>through</u> each of His disciple's lives. In other words, Jesus reproduced Himself in each of His disciples through training and impartation. Then they went out and "turned the world upside down" in a matter of just two generations. The followers of The Way had The Way inside of them!

God is after discipleship. He is after men and women who will train and disciple men and women, until they in turn are mature enough to go forth and become disciplers.

There must be a Noah to impart the ways of God to a Ham, Shem, or Japheth. There must be a Jesse and a Samuel to teach a young David. There must be an older David to impart wisdom to a young Solomon. There must be an Elijah to walk with a young Elisha and pass along a double portion of his anointing. There must be a Paul to father and impart wisdom and direction to Timothy. The purposes of God have not changed.

You must spread the gospel. You must train up those around you to spread the gospel. Look for the relationships that God has ordained as unique for your life, and begin to connect with those people on a day by day and week by week basis! With our generation, it is no longer about church meetings with a special speaker or church programs. The church must get out of its four walls and into the communities and coffee houses. "What's interesting about Generation X is that they are looking for fathering and mentoring," says Phil Buekler, another leader who has made an impact on the lives of many spiritual sons and daughters, including me. "There is a deep spiritual significance, a plus factor that this generation can bring. But they need mentoring."

There is a principle that what we value most, we lack the most. Take gold or diamonds for example. The less there is of it, the more it is treasured. Apply this to our generation. We have lacked solid, family relationships. We have lacked the formation under godly parents, and the intimacy and vulnerability found in loving, caring relationships. And what we have lacked the most as an entire generation is what we most value and most need.

THERE IS A DEEP SPIRITUAL SIGNIFICANCE, A PLUS FACTOR THAT THIS GENERATION CAN BRING. BUT THEY NEED MENTORING.

Phil shared some insight into actual Biblical strategy with me that I'd like to pass on with my own comments before closing this chapter. Both Jesus and the apostle Paul incorporated the elements of these five phases and saw good fruit as a result.

First, the modeling phase. This is defined as the mentor does it ("it" can be defined as whatever kind of ministry, gifting, or practical discipleship you are passing along) and the apprentice is exposed to it and watches from a distance. As Jesus began his earthly ministry he stretched out his hands and healed the sick, as His disciples just watched. At this point He hadn't yet even chosen His twelve, though He was probably watching closely as to which men from the crowd were the most interested in what He was doing.

Second, the mentoring phase. This is defined as the mentor doing the task, and the apprentice being right with the mentor to watch more intently. This took place after Jesus had chosen His twelve and they gathered around and started actively watching what He was doing, and listened to Him more intently as He addressed them personally and explained a bit more about what He was doing.

Third, the monitoring phase. This is defined as the apprentice doing the work, and the mentor close by watching and making any encouraging, helpful, or suggestions alongside the apprentice. Here remember Jesus asking His disciples to give the crowd something to eat. He started the process off, and handed them the work to do, and watched as the food was multiplied in their hands, not His. Sometimes Jesus would watch and then later answer questions when He was alone with the twelve. "Teacher…why…?"

Fourth, the commissioning phase. This is defined as the apprentice now given full responsibility to do the task on his/her own, without even the mentor present. Jesus at one point sent out His twelve along with others in groups of two and they went out and healed the sick, proclaimed the Kingdom, and cast out demons in His name. Later they came and reported to Him what they had done.

Fifth and lastly, the multiplying phase. This is defined as the disciple becoming the discipler. The apprentice becomes the mentor to others. Some would call this multiplication, and this is the ultimate desire in the heart of God for our generation.

Young, experienced, mature leaders discipling their own age group and mentoring them to stronger places in their walks with God.

SPEAK, DON'T STRIKE

One of the greatest tragedies today in the church is the lack of understanding within the older generation of their true role in mentoring. Many of you reading this who are older and "experienced" in ministry will need to take a moment and repent. Repent for what? For the past mistakes you have made in relating to the next generation by thinking that they must follow in the same way that you walked.

You see, the key for our generation is that we need to find our own path. In the previous chapter of this book we discussed the zeal/wisdom combination. It is imperative that we as the younger generation receive wisdom from our elders, but we also need time to digest and perhaps disagree with some of the messages we're hearing. That's why small groups with opportunities for discussion work great for us. We love to be able to respond and even criticize things we hear, not to reject the truth, but to hear someone affirm the love and concern they have for us in spite of it, which to us is more relevant in some cases than the truth being taught. In the past generation, people valued truth above relationships, which is why long sermons or speeches worked so well. We value relationships, which is why the need is there for people to drop their program mentality and just hang out with us for coffee or in internet chat rooms.

We need time to spend in prayer, sifting through the guidance and the advice to find the meat in it and discard the bones. As elders, don't despise the discarding of the bones; understand that while we value the training and the ways you have done things in the past, we need to absorb the message and come up with our own methods of doing things for the future.

Honestly, it has always been this way. For an interesting study, look at the life of Moses and the two instances of bringing water from the rock in the wilderness. Early in his ministry, God gave him a staff, which was a symbol of the gifts of the Spirit at work in his life. The staff held the miraculous power of God. Many leaders today are given gifts and talents from God, and those gifts and talents are provided for the blessing of the Body of Christ. In the first case of the water from the rock, God told Moses to strike the rock with his staff, and water would come forth. Moses was in his early, more radical days of listening to

MANY LEADERS PURSUE THEIR PROGRAMS AND THEIR MINISTRIES WITHOUT THE FRESH DIRECTION FROM THE LORD

the Lord, and his instant obedience in the exact way of God for deliverance led to a miraculous pouring forth of the water from a rock. He listened and instantly obeyed.

Later in his ministry, when habits of the flesh and more traditional ways were a part of his life, the children of Israel needed water again. God told him to <u>speak</u> to the rock this time, and water would pour forth. Instead of speaking to the rock Moses <u>struck</u> it. Water still came forth; God honored his more traditional approach, but then chastised him and that one mistake cost him from entering the promised land. Why was it "more traditional?" Because he knew it would work. It had worked in the past, in fact the staff in his hand always produced results when mixed with faith. He didn't have to obey the fresh word of the Lord to see his ministry work.

Do you see? The older Moses, more set in his ways of 'doing ministry', had settled into a habit of the flesh, and instead of the days of instant, radical obedience to the voice of the Lord, he decided to do the miracle through a known method, a method he knew would work. The staff in his hand was a symbol of the power of the Spirit at work in his life. Many leaders pursue their programs and their ministries without the fresh direction from the Lord, and though their approaches "work" in natural terms, there remains a reckoning before God because ultimately ministry must be performed under obedience, which is better than sacrifice.

This is a warning to all the older generation of leaders out there. Are you still radical, going on your knees to seek the face of God as to how to "do ministry," or have you settled into habits of the flesh, ways of doing things that you know "work," but may not be the fresh ways that God desires for the current situation? As for mentoring, some of your ways of doing ministry may relate to your apprentices, but not all of them will. Give the younger generation a chance to accept and reject, to approve and disapprove, depending on the fresh voice of the Lord for their own unique calling and direction.

FISHING NETS AND FLEXIBLE FOUNDATIONS

One of the greatest moves of the Spirit, one that you don't hear so much about but is taking place all around you, is the move of 'net-making'. Yep, Christ is going fishing, and He's building the Net. It is the net that will hold the harvest which is approaching. Satan's counterfeit is "networking," but Christ's reality is "net-making."

Every one of us needs each other. The young need the old, and the old need the young. What God is after in these days is relationships. Yes! That's the secret! Relationships who treat each other with respect and love, coupled at times with correction and prayer for character changes, of course. He's building a net of family members from all over the world. Various individuals with different giftings and callings, backgrounds, and systems of belief within the Body are uniting, slowly but surely, until we will all function and work together to the building up of the Body in love, just as Paul points out in Ephesians chapter 4. It's happening with leadership, as various camps are deciding to lay aside their differences and come together, hand in hand, and work together toward the harvest.

John Wesley was a strict Armenianist (one who holds staunchly to the free-will choice of man in salvation) who disagreed with any Calvinist (one who upholds God's sovereignty and election in the salvation of a soul). But nearing the end of his life, he softened in his attitude, and saw that he could work together with others of varying degrees of beliefs in Christendom. He was indeed a Moses who learned to be flexible in his foundational doctrines for the sake of love and unity.

One startled Calvinist, who accepted Wesley's offer to work together, changed in his attitude when Wesley said, "Are you my brother? Then clasp your hand in mine and we will work together for the sake of the gospel. Show me 100 men who are sold out to God, and I'll show you a group that will change the world."

God is after heart-knit, Spirit-led relational teamwork. And the teams are comprised of family members of various ages and maturity on the same side, united against one common foe; a foe who can be defeated, for, "One little word will fell him" as the reformation hymn from Luther goes. It isn't that we all are going to agree with each other's theology: no, it doesn't come that way. True unity in heart and spirit is when we can lay down, at the door, all of our disagreements, and concentrate on the issues we do agree on: Jesus Christ, and Him crucified. The apostle Paul had serious disagreements with other theologians of his day, who wanted to make believers become circumcised. The truth was, the new creation in Christ puts all other theological differences aside, and should cause us to walk in humility and not pride. As he put it, *"God forbid that I should boast in anything, except in the cross of our Lord Jesus Christ, through which the world has been crucified to me, and I to the world. For neither is circumcision anything, nor uncircumcision, but a new creation." Galatians 6:14-15.* To put it another way, Dr. Lance Wonders, one of my spiritual mentors, once taught me, "In essentials, unity. In non-essentials, liberty. In all things, charity."

Jesus doesn't care if your doctrine is in proper order, He's after your heart disposition. A friend of mine once spoke to a missionary friend of his, who told him, "Lord, I'll go anywhere, except South America (he didn't personally ever want to travel to South America) to serve you." Guess where God sent him? South America. He complained, "But Lord, I don't want to go there. I don't agree with all their doctrine." In the stillness of his heart, the Lord spoke. "I don't agree with all your doctrine either, but I don't have a problem with you." Needless to say, he went, and became a great blessing to the people of his region.

A VISIT TO THE WOODSHED

Correction is a curious thing in the Kingdom, especially among the fields of the fatherless. The truth is, only the Holy Spirit has the authority, the right, and the commission to bring correction in righteousness, when it needs to be administered in the realm of spiritual maturity. But God will call others to speak the truth in love to you, who have earned a right to do so by their relationship to you, whom you respect and will listen to, and others who will pray that changes will be made properly in your life and character as directed by God's Spirit.

This being said, I've had several encounters over the years by various friends in the Kingdom who have helped to sow seeds of transformation. They confronted me in areas and were instruments in the Lord's hands to bring a rod of correction and conviction through the Holy Spirit. I remember one such encounter a few years ago through the leadership of a godly father and mother in the faith.

"BOY, YOU LOOK LIKE YOU JUST CAME OUT OF THE WOODSHED."

I entered their Bible training center, and spent my first year making mistake after mistake. I'll never forget one afternoon as I was called into the office of this man and woman of God. They began the session by pointing out a few positive aspects of my calling and ministry. They then offered some areas for prayer and consideration, areas that needed some change and transformation. When I walked out of their office that day, a friend and fellow Bible school student happened to be standing there and he remarked, "Boy, you look like you just came out of the woodshed." And so I had. God my Father had given me a double dose of tough love.

HE BELIEVES IN YOU

Young people, humble yourself before the hand of God and recognize your need for a mentor! Ask the Holy Spirit to point out several potential mentors in your life, as well as a timetable to work with them, and then approach them and ask them to consider relating to you in a "special" way for a season.

A great illustration in the ways of mentoring is from the classic novel and film, <u>The Count of Monte Cristo</u>. A young man, framed for a crime he didn't commit, is enslaved in a dark prison for the rest of his life. He is full of vengeance; revenge is the only thing on his mind. In a remarkable turn of events, he builds a relationship with an old priest in the prison. The old man, an old warrior and statesman as well as a priest, takes the young man under his wing. He trains him in weapons and sword fighting, teaches him how to read and write, and instructs him how to carry himself with dignity and pride. He passes on what he knows, and allows the young man to learn to think deeply on his own. At this point in the story, the young man is an agnostic (he later becomes a believer). A key moment happens as the old man dies in the prison. He shares about God.

"But I don't believe in God," says the young man, now trained and ready for the next phase of his life.

"That's alright. He believes in you."

The last words of the old mentor ring true today for our generation. For the man who became the Count of Monte Cristo, those words eventually turned him into a man who consecrated his heart to God. Coaches, leaders, Moses' and Miriam's, no matter what your age, there is an entire generation all around you who are screaming for godly relationships! Look for the potential leaders in your midst, and begin to train and release them to go further than you would have gone.

A large portion of my own calling is evangelistic, and once I was asked to train students of a Bible college in Kazakstan for one week on the subject of evangelism and then take them out to evangelize in a village and plant a new church there. As I was preparing the teaching for my opening session at the school, the Holy Spirit spoke these haunting words to me:

"The Church as we know it is only one generation away from extinction."

Can you grasp this? In other words, if all the Christians, or followers of The Way, simply decided to stop sharing their faith and training the next generation, Christianity would become extinct. "Christianity is only one generation away from extinction" He implied. How vital is it to remember that if we don't raise up and release our current generation, we can have no expectation that they will raise up themselves.

The whole final chapter of Joshua is a great reminder to us of the importance of passing along the ways of God which we have learned, and a warning to us if we fail in this mission. If every believer decided to stop sharing their faith and fulfilling Matthew 28's charge to disciple the nations, our faith would extinguish itself by the dying of the last Christian, since no Christian can become a Christian by natural birth.

"And Israel served the Lord all the days of Joshua and all the days of the elders who survived Joshua, and had known all the deeds of the Lord which He had done for Israel." Joshua 24:31. "Then Joshua the son of Nun, the servant of the Lord, died at the age of one hundred and ten. And all the generation also were gathered to their fathers; and there arose another generation after them who did not know the Lord, nor yet the work which He had done for Israel." Judges 2:8,10.

It isn't enough for you to just continue to experience God's presence in a church setting. The calling of our Joshua Generation is unique: to pour their lives into countless others who will carry on long after we're gone.

"Moses had trained Joshua to be his successor, but Joshua and the elders were too busy conquering the Canaanites to train their own successors, to thoroughly ground new leaders in the faith of Israel," writes Spiros Zodhiates in his commentary on Joshua chapter 24. "As a result, the next generation succumbed to Canaanite idolatry. God's people are always just one generation away from apostasy. Therefore, we must train our young to walk in the fear of the Lord today before they become the leaders of tomorrow."[54]

And a whole generation is crying out, like the Count of Monte Cristo, "we don't believe in God." But the purpose of this book is to ignite you as a messenger to your own generation and spread this truth: He believes in you.

GRASPING THE PASSING BATON

"Give me where to stand, and I will shake the earth."

— *Archimedes*

"Then Joshua said to the people,

"Consecrate yourselves, for tomorrow

the Lord will do wonders among you."

— *Joshua 3:5*

PASSING THE BATON

In God's unique timetable, always watch for one thing: the death of God's old regime of leadership. It is usually a sign in the Spirit that the time has arrived for the new leadership to arise and go forth in the Spirit.

For example, when God was preparing His young warriors to go forth and cross the Jordan, He was working on Joshua. Moses was the one who was called to train the man of God. Joshua spent much time with Moses, accompanying him up the mountaintop when he went to meet with God. Joshua spent much time in the presence of the Lord as well, stealing away at every opportunity into the tabernacle to sit in the Lord's presence.

There came a day when God called Moses to commission Joshua. Still, the ordained time for Joshua to arise had not yet come. There was a further alignment necessary in the Spirit realm. The event that signaled to Joshua it was time to arise and cross over was the death of Moses. In Joshua, the first chapter, we read of God's command to Joshua: *"Moses, my servant, is dead. Now arise."*

YOU HAVE A PART TO PLAY IN THE FINAL UNFOLDING DRAMA OF THE WORLD AND THE CHURCH THEREIN

You are the Joshua Generation. God has destined you for greatness. You have a part to play in the final unfolding drama of the world and the church therein. The crucial time in the Spirit is now. Soon, probably over the next few years, some of the great men and women of God who were used in the past are going to pass on to glory; in so doing, they will pass the baton to you and me. Men and women, leaders and members of the previous generation, will pass away or be martyred.

Watch for them to die and go home to be with the Lord. Each will pass on their particular kind of anointing and call for an awaiting generation to go forth and carry the banner in the last days.

It has always been so. God has many times used the death of an individual to signal the end of a season, reign, or ministry. Look at David. Most scholars call the period when David and Solomon were on the throne "the golden age of the kingdom." In Acts 8, the scripture tells us, *"David fulfilled the call of God for his generation, and then slept with his fathers."* That was it. He did what he was called to do, and then he died. His son Solomon rose up and furthered the Kingdom by stretching her borders and building the Temple, and thus experienced the glory of God in a tangible way. David was never allowed to build what Solomon built in his day and generation. So the next generation of that day took the Kingdom further than the previous by their obedience to God.

"Moses My servant is dead; now therefore arise, cross this Jordan, you and all this people." Joshua 1:2. As Moses died, the old generation of leadership passed away, and the baton was passed. If you are reading this book, you are alive. That means you are called to affect your generation with the gospel and then die. Someday you too will pass on into the realm of eternity and pass the baton of your anointing to the next generation.

Elijah was a prophet, mightily anointed of God. And his young trainee, Elisha was desirous in a good way of receiving Elijah's anointing. He was determined. He followed him onward, boldly pressing in, even when Elijah encouraged him to stop. He went on, past Gilgal, past Bethel, crossing the Jordan, until he reached the place of Elijah's departure. *"I pray thee, let a double portion of thy spirit rest upon me."* 2 Kings 2:9.

Soon Elijah is translated into heaven by chariots of fire and Elisha catches the mantle of Elijah. He goes forth and does exactly double the number of miracles of his predecessor. Elisha was so anointed that even after he had died a dead child touched his bones and came to life. There had been a passing of the baton.

This is what is coming to the earth. God is fixing to pour out His Spirit in such a way that those who thirst after Him and hunger for His anointing will capture the mantle and go forth in signs and wonders under an unlimited anointing. In the Old Covenant, you could believe for the double portion anointing, but in the New Covenant, we have the promise of the fullness of the very Spirit of Christ who said, *"greater works than these shall you do"* and who ministered in the Spirit in an unlimited anointing, which He then passed on to His church on earth. Are you hungry? Are you looking to catch the mantle as it falls from heaven? Are you ready to fast and pray with your whole heart for an unlimited anointing to fulfill His calling in your life?

Many thousands of you will. You teens will begin to stand up in your school yards and around your flagpoles under an evangelistic anointing and pray the truth. You twenty-and-thirty-somethings will dare to walk down the most drug-infested corners of your cities, into the darkest corners and vilest holes of human existence, and pour the anointing of love and compassion that will save many. You mentors will dare to begin to open your eyes and give your time and blood, sweat, and tears to train and release those around you to go farther than you.

You will be bold and pray for gangs and pimps, poor people on the streets, or rich and wealthy people in their posh condos and homes. You will stand on beaches, on street corners, in alleys, and in all sorts of locations, and proclaim the Word of God through words and love in action. You will arise in the middle of an airplane ride, or on a bus, or a subway, and preach the truth as it is in Jesus, and many will be saved. You will love people and pray for their felt needs and open doors of truth for them to know God. You will dare to believe God to show forth the signs of the Kingdom; you will speak with new tounges, lay hands boldly on sick bodies and see them recover, speak to dead bodies and witness their resurrection from the dead. The list will go on.

YOU MUST TAKE RESPONSIBILITY TO GO FORTH IN THE LORD'S NAME; NO ONE IS GOING TO TAKE THE INITIATIVE FOR YOU

This is your hour! The time to favor you, the set time, has come. "*Cry loudly, do not hold back, raise your voice like a trumpet, and declare to My people their transgression, and to the house of Jacob their sins.*" Isaiah 58:1-2.

Smith Wigglesworth, a great man of God used mightily in the early twentieth century, used to say, "When the Holy Ghost does not move me, I move the Holy Ghost." In other words, stand up and get going. Initiate a work, and God will stand with you.

Abraham Lincoln once said, "Do not wait for your ship to come in. Swim out to it." Francis Bacon once remarked, "A wise man will make more opportunities than he finds." See, when David, who was a little fifteen year old shepherd boy, heard of the champion Goliath, he sensed the urgency in the Spirit realm. The scripture does not say so explicitly, but it is implicitly there. He hurried to make preparations. He removed every hindrance that would keep him down (Saul's armor) and caught the urgency of the moment. He RAN TO THE BATTLE LINE to engage the enemy, and you are called to do the same thing. Go forth as a young person; do not look at your age. God convinced Jeremiah of that. *"Then I said, 'Alas, Lord God! Behold, I do not know how to speak, because I am a youth.' But the Lord said to me, "Do not say, I am a youth. Because everywhere I send you, you shall go." Jeremiah 1:7a.* God is going to use YOU, no matter what your age or training. Have the response of Mary, a young teenage woman whom millions of people have adored for centuries because of her humble and yet bold reply to the call of God to carry the Savior, *"Behold, the female slave of the Lord; be it done to me according to your word." Luke 1:38.*

You must take responsibility to go forth in the Lord's name; **no one is going to take the initiative for you.** Abraham was one who caught the urgency of his hour of destiny. When God sent his entourage of three angels and were contemplating destroying Sodom, note how Abraham picked up the urgency of his hour in the Spirit. In Genesis 18:1-14 we have the complete story. Several passages contain action words like, "he ran" or "he hurried" or "quickly." It was the time of his promised son Isaac to be given by God. He responded in haste to the presence of the Lord, and you must do the same.

Part of this time is that of eternity being ushered in. We are in a hinge point of history right now. The youth and all aged under forty will play a major role in the coming years.

Recently on a ministry trip to Holland, a Dutch believer in the meeting was given a vision of a hinge on a door, signifying that we are at a crucial turning point in the history of the world. I began this writing with three sagas, or hinge points in history. The third of these is happening now, and this book is meant to be a guidepost on your journey to encourage you to continue forward in your walk with God, as either a Moses mentor or a Joshua apprentice.

God's heart is for the fields of the fatherless to become the fields of harvest. He's taking an entire group of bastard sons and daughters and turning them into an army of courageous soldiers for the kingdom. He's giving you your marching orders in this time. Remember the examples of Whitefield and of Rees Howells and his bible school students in WWII! Embrace the love of God as it is revealed in waves and waves through the Father and the Church as our mother. Practice new spiritual disciplines, and walk forward with teachability, zeal, humility, and spiritual vision. Young men, become fathers, and fathers, become coaches to cover and mentors to love our young generation into the Kingdom. Jedi apprentices become Jedi Knights! The force of the Holy Spirit is with you and the truth of Jesus Christ is your sword to cut the chains of the captives and set them free. An entire generation is waiting who doesn't believe in God, but He believes in them.

MOVE IT OUT!

Charles G. Finney was a young man used mightily by God in what historians call the Second Great Awakening. At a crucial point of the mid-1800's, there came an advancement known as the Industrial Revolution.

The multitudes of people who had been raised on rural farming communities were beginning to move to the larger cities. Cities became areas of great advancement. With the inventions of special machinery and technological advances such as electric light, photographic material, and manufacturing, many people began the transition.

Against this backdrop was the preaching of the gospel. Finney traveled from town to town proclaiming the truth of the gospel with power and conviction. Five hundred-thousand conversions were attributed to this single man of God.

WOULD YOU HAVE AN AWAKENING IN YOUR COMMUNITY, YOUR CHURCH, YOUR OWN LIVES? THEN BECOME THE FUEL, AND A REVIVAL FIRE WILL BE THE RESULT

It was he who said, "Would you have an awakening in your community, your church, your own lives? Then become the fuel, and a revival fire will be the result." In 1821, when he first began his ministry at about the age of thirty, he wrote of a particular moment in preaching to a packed church.

"The Spirit of God came upon me with such power that it was like opening a gun battery upon them. For more than an hour, the word of God came through me to them in a manner that I could see was carrying all before it. It was a fire and a hammer breaking the rock, and as a sword that was piercing to the dividing asunder of soul and spirit. I saw that a general conviction of sin was spreading over the whole congregation. Many of them could not hold up their heads.[55]

I tell you, in the realm of the Spirit, your time has come! Go for it!

There is an on-fire group of Catholic young people, known as the ICPE. Their group began just about ten years ago, when a small group of core leaders were praying one day. They received a prophetic word that they would be sent out to the ends of the earth. In a period of only a few years, this had happened. The Pope himself sanctioned their activities from Rome and gave them his blessing. They have ministry bases in Germany, Malta, Rome, and New Zealand. They have a catch phrase for their overseas mission teams, which are currently trotting to points in particular all over the globe. "Move it out!"

These seemingly insignificant believers turned whole regions upside-down with the gospel simply because they acted on the word of God to move forward. Finney's day is no different from our own. There is a huge technological and cultural shift happening in the West, and at this hinge point, you must have the same zeal and fervor of the young people at ICPE, move out, and become revival fuel for revival fire.

FANFARE FOR THE COMMON MAN

The original disciples were common men. Those who followed Christ and ministered to His needs were common women. *"Not many wise, not many mighty, not many noble are called, but God has chosen the weak things of the world to confound the things which are mighty, and the base things, and the things which are despised, to bring to nothing the things that are, that no flesh should glory in His sight." I Corinthians 1:26-29.*

After the day of Pentecost, Peter, James, John and the others were performing the miraculous and preaching the truth. This caused the crowds to marvel and proclaim, "Who are these men? Are these not plain fishermen?"

Peter was just a common fisherman. So were James and John, the so-named, "Sons of Thunder." George Whitefield once remarked, "I love those who thunder forth the Word as sons of thunder." I wonder what it was like for these men to thunder forth the Word on the street corners of Jerusalem. They were men who had been brought into living relationship with the King of Kings, clothed with power from on high, and commissioned to preach and demonstrate the mighty kingdom of God. You must have the same urgency inside of you that they had inside of them. Christ is as real and instantly accessible in your heart as He was when He walked and talked with James and John.

When Jesus came marching through the countryside, healing the eyes of the blind and opening the ears of the deaf, pro-claiming everywhere the gospel of the Kingdom, those who knew Him, or thought they knew Him, were led in wonder to proclaim, *"Is not this the carpenter's son?"*

In Acts 6 the work became too numerous for the original apos-tles, so they raised up men of godliness to take over the tasks of serving members of the newly blossoming church. Among them was Stephen, the Deacon who became a beacon; it was said of him in Acts 6:10 that "his wisdom was confounding the leaders" and he was just an ordinary young man. An ordinary young man, that is, with an extraordinary unlimited anointing. Like you.

WHAT WILL BE YOUR TOMBSTONE TESTIMONY?

"...and there arose another generation after them who did not know the Lord..." —Judges 2:10.

We end this journey with the same scripture which we began it with in the first chapter. What will be the testimony of our gen-eration? Will it have the same ironic twist as this one did? The generation of young men and women in Judges is long dead, their bones long decayed in the ground. Their testimony is sealed on the pages of scripture, and written on the tombstones in the corridors of time. *They knew not the Lord.* Yet you, as part of your own generation, have a unique responsibility to rise up, and with courage in your veins, live every day and every breath for the glory of the One who died, who rose again, and who lives within you.

At the outbreak of the American Revolutionary war, General Washington's troops were outnumbered and out-gunned. The closing months in the fall of 1776 took their toll. The chills of

THESE ARE THE TIMES THAT TRY MEN'S SOULS

winter were wearing on Washington's troops, many of whom lacked even proper shoes and were suffering frostbite. It looked like all hope was lost for the battered and sick army. In the midst of this seeming hopelessness, Thomas Paine took up his pen and ink in his tent one night among the troops and wrote these startling words, published in his work called, <u>The Crises</u>.

"These are the times that try men's souls. The summer soldier and the sunshine patriot will, in this crises, shrink from the service of their country; but he that stands it *now*, deserves the love and thanks of man and woman. Tyranny, like hell, is not easily conquered; yet we have this consolation with us, that the harder the conflict, the more glorious the triumph. What we obtain too cheap, we esteem too lightly. Heaven knows how to put a proper price upon its goods."

As each of the war-torn soldiers in Washington's army read these words in their tents with trembling, frostbitten fingers on the cold nights leading up to December 1776, something of a fresh fire was lit in their hearts. They began to burn once again for passion for the cause of freedom, and after a remarkable victory as Washington crossed the Delaware river on Christmas eve, the battle weary began to forge a campaign of victory against the enemies' tyranny. Later in the war John Adams wrote to his wife Abigale these words with the same ruthless spirit of victory in them, "we must trifle no more." And this, dear reader, is your challenge today. Desperate times as these call for desperate measures: desperate measures of concentration, commitment, and consecration. These days in which you live are the

LORD, WE WENT...

times that try men's souls. The harder the conflict, the more glorious the triumph. *"Then Joshua said to the people, 'Consecrate yourselves, for tomorrow the Lord will do wonders among you.'"* Joshua 3:5.

The valiant men and women of the Revolutionary war are long dead, but their testimonies still speak. What will your tombstone testimony be?

On an ancient mosaic wall hanging, found in a crypt in one of the oldest surviving first-century tombs in Jerusalem, is a unique picture. It shows a sailing vessel, leaving its port, and heading out into a vast unknown territory of blue water. The mast is at full sail, and the tiny inhabitants barely recognizable. At the bottom the inscription reads, "Lord, we went."

Will this be your testimony at the last day? With all you have to give, go forth. Obey the last words of Christ before His ascension. Go into all the world, and preach the gospel to every creature. May it be said of you, on your tombstone, "Lord, he went", or, "Lord, she went."

The baton has passed from the previous generation to yours. The older leadership will mentor you, then step aside and watch you soar. These hinges of history times demand a special response. Let the X that the satanic enemy has marked over your own life become a YES over your heart and step up to the challenge to defeat tyranny and stand for the Kingdom no matter what the cost for your own life. Christ's X marks the spot for you, for you are His treasure. It is time for a call to radical consecration to Christ. Your time has come to grasp the passing baton and run like hell to obtain your prize.

Can you hear the distant drum? It is beating. It is signaling the Changing of the Guard.

APPENDIX A:
MINISTRY & STUDY RESOURCES
FOR FURTHER STUDY

As I was preparing this book for publication, it occurred to me that many of you may wish to delve deeper into the many truths only touched upon in certain sections of this book. With that in mind, I pulled from my personal library a few volumes which, over the course of time, have ministered deeply to me and may do the same for you. This is by no means an exhaustive list, but is meant to be a mini-resource for you to touch deeper on themes or people I've referred to over the course of this book. May the Lord put His stamp of inner witness to any of these following works in your life to bear fruit for His name. There are ten books in each section, categorized by general theme, and in no particular order.

—the author

<u>Themes</u>: Daily Devotion, Radical Discipleship

Dietrich Bonhoeffer, <u>The Cost of Discipleship</u> (Simon & Schuster, 1959).

Hannah Whithall Smith, <u>The Christian's Secret of a Happy Life</u> (Barbour & Company, 1985).

Francois Fenelon, <u>Christian Perfection</u> (Bethany House, 1975).

Watchman Nee, <u>The Normal Christian Life</u> (Tyndale House Publishers, 1985).

C.S. Lewis, <u>Mere Christianity</u> (Macmillan Publishing Company, 1960).

J. Oswald Sanders, <u>Spiritual Leadership</u> (Moody Bible Institute, 1989).

Charles G. Finney, <u>Revival Lectures</u> (Fleming H. Revell Company).

Norman Grubb, <u>Rees Howells, Intercessor</u> (Christian Literature Crusade, 1952).

<u>John G. Lake, His Life, His Sermons, His Boldness of Faith</u> (Kenneth Copeland Publications, 1994).

Arnold Dallimore, <u>George Whitefield, Volumes I and II, *the life and times of the great evangelist of the 18th century revival*</u> (Banner of Truth, 1970 & 1980, respectively).

<u>Themes</u>: The Church and Her Purpose, Theology, and The Battle for the Earth

Peter Greig & Dave Roberts, <u>Red Moon Rising, *how 24/7 prayer is awakening a generation*</u> (Relevant Books, 2003).

Martin Scott, <u>Impacting the City, *a four-fold spiritual warfare strategy for your community*</u> (Soverign Word Publishing, 2004).

Ted Haggard, <u>The Life Giving Church</u> (Regal Books, 1998).

C. Peter Wagner, <u>Engaging the Enemy, *how to fight and defeat territorial spirits*</u> (Regal Books, 1991).

Michael L. Brown, <u>Revolution! The Call to Holy War</u> (Regal Books, 2000).

Winkie Pratney, <u>Revival, *principles to change the world*</u> (Whitaker House, 1983).

John Wimber & Kevin Springer, <u>Power Evangelism</u> (Harper Collins, 1992).

Bruce Milne, <u>Know the Truth: Revised Edition, *a handbook of Christian belief*</u> (InterVarsity Press, 1998).

George Otis, Jr., <u>The Last of the Giants, *lifting the veil on Islam and the end times*</u> (Chosen Books, 1991).

Jim Peterson, <u>Church Without Walls</u> (Navpress, the Navigators Publishing, 1992).

NOTES

1 Excerpt from a spontaneous prayer during, "Passion, the Road to One Day." A worship CD published by Sparrow Records, Brentwood, Tennessee.

2 –Ralph Waldo Emerson.

3 Ron Luce, Inspire the Fire, Creation House, 1994.

4 Adapted from an article entitled "Strategies to Attract, Manage and Retain the Next Generation" by Rebecca Ryan, 2001. Published as public domain on her website.

5 John Yemma, adapted from, The Future of Youth Ministry", July 18, 1991.

6 Rick Joyner, adapted from The Morning Star Bulliten, January 1996.

7 adapted from an email by Irene Mederos, The Voice of Fire Prophetic Ministries, 1998.

8 Greg Behr, The Content of Our Character: The Voices of Generation X. March 1999. The entire document can be downloaded from their website: contentofourcharacter.org

9 Excerpt from, "Jesus is Coming!" journal entry on the Passion Network website, by Louie Gigleio. Further info on upcoming Passion worship events is available on their website, www.passionnow.org

10 Dr. Michael L. Brown, Revolution! The Call to Holy War. Regal Books, 2000.

11 David Works, "The Torch Has Passed" email dated Sunday, August 8, 1999.

12 Bobby Conners, adapted from an email message entitled, "Generation YES!", January 12, 2000.

13 Adapted from an email message by Bobby Conner, Bobby Conner Ministry, 1999.

14 Adapted from an email vision called, "Sons of Glory" by Catherine Brown, West Kilbride, Scotland, Feb.2000.

15 Adapted from an email from Cindy Jacobs, Generals of Intercession, November 30, 1999.

16 Adapted from Bob Jones and Keith Davis, Shepherd's Rod 2001, October 9, 2000.

17 Adapted from an article labeled, "Generation Miraculous" by Todd Bentley, Fresh Fire Ministries, 2000.

18 Adapted from an article by Dave Bodine, Northwest Revival Network, May 25, 2000.

19 Luther's Works, vol.24, 1961, pg 224.

20 Arnold Dallimore, "George Whitefield" Volume 1. The Banner of Truth Trust, 1970.

21a Luther's Works, vol.24, 1961, pg 417.

21b Taken from, Red Moon Rising: how 24-7 prayer is awakening a generation. This is a portion of Pete's amazing poetic discipleship writing called appropriately, "The Vision", page 121. To order this book or learn more about this stirring movement of prayer & outreach warriors, go to: www.24-7prayer.com.

22 Time Magazine, June 9, 1997 issue, Generation X Gets Real, pg. 68.

23 Quoted from a Voice of America broadcast in 1995.

24 George Barna, Generation Next, Regal Books, Ventura, California, 1995, pp. 18-20.

25 David Plaistad, quoted in an introduction to, Romans Rewrite, pp. 2.

26 Glen Charles, adapted from a seminar on Generation X at YWAM.

27 John Stott, "Between 2 Worlds." Eerdmans Publishing Co, Grand Rapids, Michigan, 1982.

28 The Orange County Weekly, Cover Story, August 20, 1992.

29 Ibid.

30 Ibid.

31 Excerpt of lyrics from, Mike and the Mechanics, "The Living Years" song.

32 David Plaistad, quoted in an introduction to, Romans Rewrite, pp. 2.

33 John L. Nickalls, Journal of George Fox, Society of Friends, 1985, p.117-122.

34 Juan Carlos Ortiz, Call to Discipleship, pp, 89. Logos International, 1975.

35 Excerpt from a Radio Broadcast of Voice of America, 1994.

36 Documented from a radio broadcast from Voice of America, 1995.

37 Juan Carlos Ortiz, "Call to Discipleship." Pp. 52, Bridge Publishing Inc., 1975.

38 Arnold Dallimore, "George Whitefield" Volume II. The Banner of Truth Trust, 1970.

39 Ibid.

40 Ibid.

41 Ibid.

42 Norman Grubb, Rees Howells, Intercessor, pp. 208. Christian Literature Crusade, 1952.

43 Ibid, pp. 210.

44 Ibid, pp 212.

45 Ibid, pp. 257.

46 By Ernest Shurtleff, published by Mrs. Charles E. Cowman, Streams in the Desert, Vol.2, Welch Publishing Company, 1966.

47 Illustrations Unlimited, James S. Hewett, editor. Tyndale House, Wheaton, Illinois, 1988.

48 The Revell Bible Dictionary, pp. 352, Baker Books, Grand Rapids, Michigan,1990.

49 Matthew Henry's Commentary, page 1174. Hendrckson Publishers, Peabody, Massachusetts, April 1992.

50 The Diary of Howell Harris, in the beginning of his ministry. He introduced open air style preaching before Wesley or Whitefield, 1730 at the age of 25, in Wales. Quoted from, "The Life and Times of George Whitefield" by Arnold Dallimore.

51 From an old bookmark. Referenced in, "Streams in the Desert" by Mrs. Robert Coleman.

52 Francois Fenelon, Christian Perfection, pp. 22-23.Bethany House Publishers, 1975.

53 Mrs. Charles E. Cowman, Streams in the Desert, Volume 2, pp. 154. Welch Publishing Company, 1966.

54 Spiros Zodhiates, The Hebrew-Greek Key Study Bible, note on Joshua 24:31, pp.326. New American Standard Edition, AMG Publishers, 1990.

55 Helen Wessel, The Autobiography of Charles G. Finney, pp. 57. Bethany House Publishers, 1977.

APPENDIX B:

ABOUT THE
AUTHOR

REV. CARL WESLEY ANDERSON, JR., M.DIV.

 Carl Wesley Anderson, Jr. is founder of Born to Blaze Ministries and President of a tentmaking corporation, Princess Bride Cinematic Videography. Carl has had the privilege of ministering and traveling extensively throughout the U.S., UK, Europe and Asia taking God's call to young adults. Carl holds a B.A. in speech communication and a Masters of Divinity.

Carl began preaching at the age of 17 in various Lutheran church settings. By age 20, he was about to graduate from Concordia College when he saw his need for a deeper personal relationship with Jesus Christ. Carl immediately committed his life to Christ and soon after received the baptism of the Holy Spirit—transforming Carl as well as his ministry—now being able to preach from personal experience as well as a balanced theological perspective. Licensed and ordained in 1994, Carl holds credentials through Harvest Network International. After spending three years in personal prayer and study, Carl acquired a Masters of Divinity degree from ACTS International Bible School. Carl's ministry experience includes ministering with Christian International, ICPE, and Youth With a Mission in Germany and Ireland.

In Europe and the U.K., Carl has held street preaching out-reaches in various cities, trained saints in evangelization, and ministered in Roman Catholic, charismatic Protestant, and Evangelical ministry groups. Carl has also spent time in the Muslim nations of Uzbekistan and Kazakhstan with The Bridge International, helping to train new converts in evangelism and the gifts of the Holy Spirit.

BORN TO BLAZE MINISTRIES

Carl founded Born to Blaze Ministries in 1991 as an international outreach *to call people to repentance and inspire believers to passionate discipleship.* There is a stirring in the heart of Born to Blaze to serve and support the work of leaders in the body of Christ around the world—to add fire to what leaders are already doing. Whether it be teaching, training, giving practical help, preaching, inspiring the next generation, or even helping to host outreaches and combined events, Born to Blaze adds its giftings where needed. The goal is building up the Body of Christ and planting new passion for the things of God. Carl is assisted by his wife Sarah Elizabeth, and they co-write "Blazing Oil", a teaching newsletter published quarterly, providing ongoing teachings and Spirit-directed exhortations. Together with their three children, Carl and Sarah

make their home in Minneapolis, Minnesota. Born to Blaze Ministries can be contacted by emailing **info@bornto-blaze.com** or visiting **www.borntoblaze.com**.

BORN TO BLAZE

MINISTRIES

WE WANT TO HEAR FROM YOU

HOW HAS THIS BOOK CHANGED OR INSPIRED YOU?

Write your testimony in the space below and mail this page to: Born to Blaze Ministries, P.O. Box 46105, Plymouth, Minnesota, 55446, U.S.A. OR email us at info@borntoblaze.com.

❏ Yes, Born to Blaze can reprint my testimony.

❏ HOW DID THIS BOOK COME INTO YOUR HANDS?

❏ YES! I WANT TO JOIN THE RANKS OF THE NEW GUARD.
Please add me to your mailing list.

_____
Name

_____
Address

_____
City   State / Country   Zip

_____
Email   Telephone

For radical discipleship materials and additional information, or to order more copies of this book for your friends or ministry relationships,
VISIT OUR WEB SITE AT www.borntoblaze.com